PRISMS

Identifying Gifts that Reveal God's
Creative Spirit

Joyce Madsen & Clair Woodbury

The Congregational Life Centre

Prisms is published by:

    The Congregational Life Centre
    #1405, 5328 Calgary Trail,
    Edmonton AB T6H 4J8

For permission, or to share any comments or questions, contact:

    Joyce Madsen & Clair Woodbury
    Congregational Life Centre
    #1405, 5328 Calgary Trail,
    Edmonton AB T6H 4J8

    Phone: 780 619-0386
    e-mail: joyceandclair@congregationallife.com
    Internet: www.congregationallife.com

The cover design and interior art is by Robert Woodbury. Swirling galaxies convey the energy released when we allow the full range of our gifts to flourish. The full spectrum of colours depict the abundance of gifts generated by God's love as it flows through us to others.

ISBN: 0-9688358-2-1

Contents

This resource is dedicated
to the members of our
Congregational Life Centre Board
who have journeyed with us
as we sought to explore our gifts
and put them at the service of the church:
Carol Allen, David Barnum, Margaret Hetherington, Debbie Hubbard,
Scott Montgomery, Linda Paddon, Molly Platts, and Leslie Whitehead.

Our thanks to those who volunteered to read the manuscript or test our Prisms instruments and have offered so many helpful suggestions. Thanks to Summer Bozohora whose artistic sensitivity helped shape the presentation. Our special thanks to Heather Marshall for once again editing our final draft and giving us such sage advice.

Prisms

We cannot see light. It may be all around us, but light itself is invisible. When you shine a beam of light through a prism — a triangular piece of glass — white light turns into a rainbow of colour.

We cannot see God, though God's love is all around us. That love becomes visible to us when those around us exercise their God-given gifts to reach out to us. The qualities of leadership, planning, communicating, caring, discernment, spirituality, mentoring, and artistic creative — each is a gift that reveals the love of God.

That is why this resource is called *Prisms* — it reveals the gifts that reveal God.

Joyce Madsen and Clair Woodbury

Prisms

1. A Spiritual Prism

"You are a gifted individual!" When you realize this, you have access to a new way of being a Christian. Too often in the past, being a Christian meant following someone else's model of how to relate to God, how to relate to others, and where to put your energy. That is changing today. We relate to God in a way that flows naturally out of the spiritual practices that fit us best. It is our gifts that guide how we contribute to the welfare of others and where we put our energy.

We wrote this book because we want individuals to have a clear understanding of what constitute their strongest gifts. We have a deep conviction that it is precisely these gifts that God wants us to use and develop to their maximum potential.

There is a great freedom in going with your gifts — sensing a call to do what you do best and be even better at it than you ever have been. Paul wrote to the Galatians, "For freedom Christ has set us free," (Galatians 5:1) and "You were called to freedom, brothers and sisters." (Gal. 5:13) If he were alive today he would be writing those same words to churches all over — it is freedom to which you have been called, the freedom to use the gifts God has given you, because that is precisely why you have been given special gifts, that they might be used. Paul would remind us of Jesus' words, "No one after lighting a lamp puts it under a bushel basket . . . Let your light shine." (Matt. 5:15-16) We shine when we develop our gifts and use them to the best of our ability.

This book is also for congregations. When a congregation recognizes where the real gifts of its people lie, the benefits begin to appear right away. People finish tasks with more energy than when they began. They develop a deep sense of satisfaction. They relate to others with a smile on their face and love in their heart.

As you read through this resource, you might want to have a candle burning nearby. You have a light that needs to shine, just like that candle. Jesus was certainly clear, and we are too, that the task God has given every person is to release the light their gifts can provide for the world God loves.

Gifts are For Giving, not Plugging In

We developed *Prisms* because we have seen too many congregations held back by old ways of being the church — more intent on plugging people into vacant positions than bringing out each individual's true gifts for ministry.

Love in your heart wasn't put there to stay,
Love isn't love 'till you give it away.

Congregations all too often greet newcomers with the question, "Which of our groups would you like to join, or is there a committee that you would like to serve on?" This often results in people being plugged into slots where they do not really fit because there is a vacancy in the church's structure.

We propose a 180 degree turn on that approach — a complete about face. We would like to see congregations develop a relationship with a newcomer to the point where that person's gifts and needs become known — whether, for example, they have come for healing or for helping. If it is for healing, the gifts of the congregation can be brought into play to meet that need. If it is for helping, the question is then, "What ministry do you have gifts and a passion for, and how can we help you carry out that call from God?"

Recognizing and supporting people's gifts may well require a congregation to drop some committees that did good work in the past but whose focus is no longer contributing to the current direction. When a congregation builds on people's gifts, it eliminates conflict over what activities or programs to keep and which to leave behind. You keep the programs that make use of people's gifts, and drop those that don't. A congregation's focus must change as the needs of its people and those in the surrounding community change. In this era of scarce resources, scarce funds, and scarce volunteer time, focusing on essentials is crucial. We are told that the key to being a successful retail outlet is "location, location, location." The key to being the church today is "focus, focus, focus."

This Prisms approach requires a real change of heart on the part of congregational leaders because the majority of ministries will be carried on outside the church. The 21st century congregation has a crucial role to play in preparing and supporting people for a ministry at their place of work, in their family setting, in the organizations where they are volunteers, or with friends.

Some congregations will have ministries that are carried out using the church building as a base. In a life-giving congregation these so-called "visible" ministries are only the "tip of the iceberg" compared to what members are contributing to their families, colleagues, and neighbours as a result of their Christian calling. The church has always known it was called to celebrate the invisible as well as the visible. Today that has become even more imperative.

Grandfathers, Grandmothers

Clair is a grandfather. That means relating to five incredible granddaughters. Joyce is a grandmother. Get her started on her four grandsons and there is no stopping her.

What is our role as grandparents? Clair's granddaughter Carys is very clear about that. "Your role is to spoil me!" Well, that is true. But there is a deeper role, and that is to encourage and bring out all the gifts that young women and young men have inside them.

For Carys it meant spotting the ability to be right on key when singing a song. Encouraging that musical ability led to sponsoring membership in the local music conservatory children's choir. Uncovering Carys' flare for the dramatic meant enrolling her in a theatre production. Observing granddaughter Paige's sketches led to buying a full set of artist's paints for her birthday. Seeing Haley's musical ability with a toy keyboard led to purchasing her a full-sized piano.

Joyce spotted a natural curiosity in Carson for understanding what was going on around him. That led to a trip to the star theatre. He was able to explain a concept of time to his mother that he had learned in a way that was beyond Grandma's comprehension. Walking with Maclean at Radium, Joyce found him asking about the various plants and natural formations. Christmas and birthday presents celebrate his interest in nature and how things grow. When three-year-old grandson Joe takes on a persona, he becomes that person, and Grandma has to relate to that persona in order to talk to him. Granddaughters. Grandsons. Fascinating potential that needs recognition and encouragement to blossom into full-blown gifts.

Is it any surprise that the key role of the church is exactly the same — to help individuals identify their spiritual gifts and to encourage their full development?

Is that not what Jesus did with those he encountered? When Jesus visited Mary and Martha, he affirmed Martha's hospitality by being there, and Mary's spirituality by affirming she was doing the right thing listening and learning. (Luke 10:38 ff). The Good Samaritan was commended for his gift of caring for the man who had been robbed and beaten (Luke 10:25 ff). Jesus affirmed those with a gift for casting out demons, even if they were capitalizing on his name in doing so (Luke 9:49-50). The examples go on and on.

Not everyone realizes where their potential lies, or what their gifts are. It is as if we are too close to see ourselves. Others, looking from the outside, are sometimes able to see something we miss. That is something Jesus did often.

Recognizing our gifts is one thing. Having the courage to go ahead and develop them is another. There is a lot of pressure on young people to "fit in." In an article in the United Church *Observer* (February 2003), author Jim Lawson points out how "leadership" has been a bad word in that denomination for the past thirty years. The emphasis on equality and everyone participating, when taken to the extreme, can result in the failure to recognize a particular gift for leadership — or any of the other gifts which make us unique. What we know is that everyone has tremendous potential, but it requires encouragement and the opportunity to develop it.

Those of us who are older grew up in the industrial era. It was a time when every service in the United Church of Canada began with singing "Holy, holy, holy." Every Roman Catholic congregation in the world did its liturgy in Latin. The Book of Common Prayer was standard fare in every Anglican service. The aim of theological colleges was to prepare clergy so they could be interchangeable with every other clergy. Individuality was a problem, fitting-in was the ideal.

Today incredible specialization in almost every profession has made complex treatment, tailor-made products, and customized services available. Is it any surprise that people expect their congregation to meet their specific needs? Churches are increasingly realizing that the old sign "Everyone Welcome" that once graced all church bulletin boards no longer applies. No one congregation has the resources to meet everyone's needs. Congregations have to specialize more and more in the particular ministries where their strengths lie in order to provide the quality of service people expect.

Good restaurants have waiters that inform people about their specialties. They know it's the dishes where they excel that will bring people back time and time again. Congregations, likewise, need to make it clear to first time visitors what their specialties are. It also means being on the lookout for lay people and clergy with gifts in those specialization areas.

Paul shared his concept of gifts with the congregation at Corinth (I Cor. 12). Our individual strengths are God-given gifts, and the church needs the gifts of many people working in harmony in order to fulfill the mission God has assigned it. It is that diversity that gives a congregation its richness. Paul also told that same congregation that the greatest gift of all was love (I Cor. 13). We believe a congregation realizes a deep unity through the common love of God shared by all, and a deep richness by sharing that love with the thousands of unique neighbours whose lives its members encounter on a daily and weekly basis.

What does it mean to love? If you love someone, you want the very best for them. You want them to become what God intends them to be, to develop their full potential, to know their gifts and to use them. To be the church means nothing more than this, but also nothing less.

Gifts are a Prism

We call this book *Prisms* because it is our belief that every gift is a prism through which we see God at work. The common form of a prism is a triangular piece of glass that transforms the white light that enters it into a band of colour. It lets you see light.

Gifts are only gifts when they are being used to give to others. That is the first insight. The second is even more important. Gifts are prisms that let us see God at work. It is in that act of giving to others that we come to know God at work through us. It is in observing giving individuals that we see God at work through them. Gifts in action are the way we know God.

We can God very clearly in children Christmas morning as they open their gifts with wide-eyed wonder. Many of us have sensed the closeness of God when we have witnessed two people giving themselves to one another in marriage or holy union. It is truer than true that it is in giving that we receive. In giving we receive the greatest gift of all, a deep sense of God's will becoming a reality through us.

A prism receives white light and reveals its component colours. Individuals see their gifts reflected through their work and relationships. In the same way, a congregation receives many individuals and helps them reveal the colour of their gifts from God. Those gifts form a rainbow of abilities that enable the congregation to be what it is intended to be.

The Presence of Passion

The movie *My Fat Greek Wedding* was a surprise hit. Low budget, strained plot, unknown star. Yet as the young couple prepared for their wedding, their passion for embracing cultural differences captured not only their families but also theatre goers everywhere. We remember Winston Churchill for his passionate use of the English language in the battle against Nazi domination of Europe. It was the passionate portrayal of Mahatma Ghandi by Ben Kingsley that gave David Lean's film *Ghandi* an enduring place in our consciousness and continues to make the case for the effectiveness of non-violent resistance.

At the Congregational Life Centre we teach a number of courses, both on the Internet and in intensive one-week sessions. Each course closes with an assignment — a paper to display participants' grasp of the subject and to explore what their new insights mean for the church and personal faith. Over the years, we have observed without fail that the papers where the words fly off the page and captivate the imagination are the ones that are written out of a passion for the subject.

> *It is the soul's duty to be loyal to its own desires. It must abandon itself to its master passion.*
> *- Rebecca West*

Clair has guided a number of students through the process of obtaining their Doctor of Ministry degree from St. Stephen's College. The ones who made it through the five-year process are those whose passion has sustained them.

It is one thing to have identified our gifts. It is another to recognize where our passions lie, so that we can apply those gifts in a way that energizes and sustains us. When we give with passion, we receive more energy from the giving than we expend. When we give without passion, the giving drains us of what little energy and passion we might have.

What we want this book to do is to help individuals perceive where their spiritual gifts lie, then develop a sense of where they have a deep passion for applying those gifts.

This book is an important resource, not just for individuals, but also for congregations. The test instrument can be used with a group of individuals in order to identify the spectrum of gifts available for the congregation to build on.

Gifts are prisms through which we see God at work. We hope this book will be a gift. May it be so.

2. Gifts

Remember the closing scene from the movie *Doctor Zhivago?* Alec Guinness plays Yuri Zhivago's brother who entered the Soviet KGB secret police and has risen high in its ranks. He is talking to the girl he thinks is the daughter of Yuri and Lara. The girl denies it, and is walking away with the young man who is her partner. Yuri's brother spots the balalaika she has strapped on her back. Yuri's brother calls out, "Tanya. Can you play the balalaika?"

"Can she play? She's an artist!" responds her companion.

"An artist? Who taught you?"

"No one taught us."

"Ah," Yuri's brother calls after her, "then it's a gift." He knows then, this is Yuri and Lara's child, but in a moment of full humanity respects her desire to live her life forward and not out of the past. It is a parable, of course, for Russia itself. He lets them go, and she walks out of the film and into our hearts to take up the challenge of building a new Russia.

"It's a gift." How many times have we heard those words? The gifted child, the gifted musician, the gifted teacher, the gifted artist.

When we see people using their God-given gifts, we see God at work. That leads directly to the question: "What are the gifts God has given me? What are the gifts God has given you?"

It is not an easy question to answer. One way to answer is to turn to a "Spiritual Gifts Inventory," of which many are available. Quite often they provide a long list of gifts that seem more fitted to slotting people into service positions in the institutional church than uncovering true areas of potential.

We want to do just the opposite — identify the spiritual gifts of individuals so that congregations can focus their energies on supporting and encouraging individuals in the use of their gifts.

We have identified eight key gifts possessed by people: leadership, planning, communicating, caring, discernment, spirituality, mentoring, and artistic creativity. Don't think of them as boxes, limiting possibilities. Think of them as doorways that open to a wider world, windows to areas of life that invite exploration.

We arrived at these eight through a combination of research, intuition and inspiration. They come out of a lifetime of participation in mainline congregations, followed by five years of research into congregational dynamics and eight years of consulting with congregations of every mainline denomination. We also reviewed twenty different spiritual gifts inventories, making lists of the gifts we knew were crucial for people's spiritual growth and for making a contribution, not just to the organized church, but to the many communities where we live and work. We chose the eight we felt were key. Then we checked that the others on our list fit under one or more of those categories.

> *Waste no more time talking about great souls and how they should be. Become one yourself!*
> *- Marcus Aurelius*

Why only eight? We could identify a hundred gifts, as some inventories do, but when there are that many they come across as confining boxes. By choosing only eight, we hope to release the imagination, not limit it.

Leadership

It was a bright and sunny day just outside Kingston, Ontario, when Combat Keener got his nickname. It was the first summer of training as signals officer cadets. Clair's squad was to occupy a little hill and defend it. Keener's squad had the task of sneaking up on them through the tall grass and attacking the position.

It was a long wait, Clair remembers. Then a couple of hundred meters away, a smoke bomb went off. A shout was heard as Keener leapt to his feet and came running — all by himself. It was Rambo, charging the machine gun nest; Clint Eastwood, taking on the bad guys all by himself. Keener hesitated, stopped, looked very perplexed, turned around, found he was all alone, and sheepishly trotted back to find out what had happened to the rest of his squad.

It turned out his buddies were fighting a grass fire that had been set off by the smoke bomb. He got the name "Combat" that evening at camp, and it stuck. Combat Keener. It was a key lesson in leadership. If you are going to lead, make sure your followers are with you.

Leaders are people who hold the vision for a community. They understand how important it is for a community to know where it is going. They are able to articulate that vision in a way that invites others to share it, and they activate a passion for achieving that vision in those around them. They bring their followers with them.

It is very easy, when faced by a multitude of demands, to lose one's sense of direction. It is the vision holders, those who know where a community is going, who provide a steadying hand on the wheel.

Leadership is a multi-faceted gift. It includes the ability to motivate, align, inspire, and encourage people. A leader needs to estimate the resources required to complete a project, recruit people with the necessary skills, share the nature of the project so that everyone is motivated, and finally, have the tenacity to stay with the project until it is completed.

"You are Peter, and on this rock I will build my church," Jesus is reported to have said to the disciple that up to that point had been known as Simon (Matt. 16:18). Jesus recognized the gift of leadership, and called it into action.

Sometimes leadership is a gift that is exercised out front, taking the initiative when no one else steps forward, tackling that tough task that others hesitate to take on. There is a strategy that outstanding leaders know almost intuitively. Start with a couple of easy tasks to get warmed up, solidify the team and gain confidence. Then tackle the hardest task while everyone is still fresh. After that, you are on your way.

Other times, leadership is exercised from behind; encouraging others, ensuring people have the equipment they need for the task, and coordinating efforts. This kind of leadership creates more leaders as people gain confidence in their ability to step out and get a job done. Enabling leadership builds relationships, signals that friendship is important, and creates a sense that "we are all in this together."

The true leader is flexible and knows when to switch from enabling leadership to directive leadership, and then back again. Most of the time, enabling leadership is the style required. When there are difficult decisions to be made and inertia to be overcome, good leaders almost intuitively know it is time to take an active role in dealing with the crisis, developing a consensus around the decision or moving directly on the problem.

Jesus demonstrated several of the leadership styles that we see today. Jesus was charismatic, yes — crowds followed him, young people were attracted to him. This, however, was not the ultimate type of leadership he depended on.

Jesus was spiritual. People felt the presence of God when they were with him. However, Jesus' leadership consisted of more than introducing people to an experience of God, important as this was.

The key style of leadership we see in Jesus is that of the visionary. He had a vision of a new society where each person was enabled to be the best that they could be. The effectiveness of his visionary leadership style can be seen in the explosion of Christianity after his death. The leader was gone, but others picked up leadership where he had left off. It is that style of leadership that is needed today.

Planning

The planners of this world are those who are clear about the vision — where the group wants to go — and can develop a strategy and tactics that will enable the group to get there. These are the people who create order out of chaos. They seem to be able to provide the labels and the questions that put things in order.

Linda Paddon is a planner. When her congregation launched its building program several years ago, she was asked to head it up. There were a thousand details to keep in mind, an overall direction to maintain, and a goal that had to be kept in sight in the middle of a flurry of activity. Linda, from the outset, did not tie herself to any specific model. She understood that being open to all of the ideas and suggestions that others made was critical to the overall success of the project. She also understood that open communication would make the difference between success and failure, so she established a process to keep the congregation informed about each and every step as the building progressed.

Linda's gift of listening without becoming defensive, making decisions that are well researched, and honouring and respecting everyone involved in the process, resulted in a very successful building program.

Jesus knew the importance of planning. "Which of you, intending to build a tower," Jesus counselled his followers, "does not first sit down and estimate the cost, to see whether he has enough to complete it?" (Luke 14:28) If you don't, Jesus implied, you will be the talk of the neighbourhood. "This fellow began to build and was not able to finish" (Luke 14:30).

When her congregation felt it was time to re-examine its focus, Linda was asked to head up that process. Planners have a keen mind for detail, and for the steps that will lead to the desired result. Planners connect resources to tasks. They spot the roadblocks that will hinder moving ahead and figure out ways to remove them. They are flexible, because they know the ways to get to the goal is not always a straight line.

Planning and Leadership are closely connected. Leadership ensures everyone knows where they are going. Planning makes sure people have everything they need for the journey. Leaders hold the vision. Planners develop strategies and tactics that will enable everyone to move toward that common destination.

Communicating

Crosley Hunter was probably 80 years old at the time. He was the guest speaker at Sydenham Street United Church in Kingston, Ontario. Clair still remembers almost every word of that sermon. The title said it all: "Great Words can be Defined only in terms of Personality." The mothers we have known define the word "mother". People like David Livingston and Robert McClure define the word "missionary". For we who are Christian, Jesus defines the word "God". It was simple, direct, emotional, and above all, memorable.

The gift of communicating is the ability to share a message with others. Some communicate through writing that captures attention and the imagination. For others this gift takes the form of story telling, spinning a narrative that awakens memories and stirs the imagination.

There is a reason God gave us two ears and one mouth — we are to do twice as much listening as talking. We can't speak to a person's need unless we know where they are coming from. We know it takes time to listen to people's stories, to hear how they perceive their situation. Sitting on one's anxieties and doing the work of listening, however, is a crucial part of the ability to communicate.

We recently heard a 45-minute sermon delivered by the pastor at Calgary's Centre Street Church. We were with the speaker every second for most of that time for one simple reason. What he said was dealing with a real issue for us and for most of the people in that 1,800 seat auditorium — the loneliness and isolation we feel because our lives have gotten too busy with work to leave room for friendship.

Jesus' gift for communicating came through his ability to encapsulate his message into parables — stories that challenge accepted ways of doing things. He also used poetry to create statements that stuck in the minds of his followers and listeners.

> Blessed are you who are poor,
> for yours is the kingdom of God.
> Blessed are you who are hungry now,
> for you will be filled.
> Blessed are you who weep now,
> for you will laugh (Luke 6:20-21).

Communication is based on common experience. When we use a word like *hot* it may recall lazy sun-baked afternoons on the beach, or the pleasant feel of heat radiating from a fireplace, the comforting taste of a hot cup of cocoa, or the painful experience of touching something that burned your hand. The context in which the word is used helps narrow down the experience, but it is ultimately our experience that gives a word meaning for us. The word *fire* conjures up very different emotions in a badly scarred burn victim than in two lovers recalling time beside a campfire.

Good communication depends on combining ideas and experiences to create a mood, a conviction, or momentum. A pianist uses the same 88 keys available to every other piano player, but the ways the sounds are combined can communicate a vast range of colours and emotions.

We all have an ability to communicate. A person with a gift for communication is able to use their creative imagination to share what they know in ways that enhance faith, create new levels of conviction, explore new ideas, or open new pathways for action.

Caring

The gift of caring involves getting to know people well enough to understand how to help develop their potential.

A friend who has the gift of caring is Carol Allen. She has been collecting furniture and dishes for people in need for years, caring for people who need a stove, a couch, a picture for their wall. It is not just about collecting and distributing stuff. For Carol, caring means getting to know people and discovering what will make their life more comfortable, richer, more secure. It is about welcoming newcomers to the country and the community. It is about letting people know that they are important.

Caring is Jim, who met newcomers at the church door with a greeting that was genuine and sincere to the point where he recognized Joyce right away the next Sunday and called her by name. Caring is Helen, taking the time to have tea with the seniors she knew. Caring is the Anglican who sat next to Joyce and opened the Book of Alternate Services to the right page for her as the service moved to different sections.

What does it mean to care? Jesus put it this way: "I was hungry and you gave me food, I was thirsty and you gave me something to drink, I was a stranger and you welcomed me" (Matt. 25:35). It is a matter of meeting people's needs.

Caring for others can happen one-on-one or in groups. It might be about fighting for justice for all, or being there for a friend who is lonely. It is one of the gifts that many possess in different ways, and the one we can share with others in any environment or community. The story of the Good Samaritan identifies a time when the gift was shared with a stranger. How we deal with emergency situations reflects how well we understand that we are our brothers' keeper.

Discernment

The gift of discernment is one part observation, one part creative imagination, and a whole lot of just walking around an issue or a challenge until the way ahead becomes clear.

Joshua had a problem. The entrance to the land the Israelites had been promised was guarded by the walled city of Jericho. Joshua gave a strange set of instructions to the Israelite army. Every day they were to go out and march around the outside of the city walls — trumpets blowing, priests in their finery, soldiers fully equipped. Imagine the heat, the flies, and all that walking. Six days they did that, and then on the seventh day, they were to walk around seven times. You can imagine those bored soldiers, slogging around the wall, eating the dust stirred up by those ahead, dodging the occasional rock or arrow flung down upon them by the city's defenders. By the time they did that much walking around the walls, they would have spotted every crack, every handhold, every weak stone, every place the guards were lax. We are told that when the final trumpet blew, taking the city was as easy as if the walls had fallen down.

Joseph Matthews, founder of a community renewal project in Chicago's black west side, always insisted on identifying at least three options before taking action. The first, he would say, is likely what you want to do. The second is what you think you ought to do. The third just may be what God wants you to do.

Discernment often means thinking outside the box. It is realizing you don't have to land on the moon in order to get there — you park the ship in orbit and take a small lander to the surface.

Discernment has a lot to do with asking the right questions. When Clair was in his second year of university, his physics professor, Doug Rodgers, said he was willing to lead a bible study group. A chemist turned missionary, Henry Burton Sharman, had developed the format. One book consisted of the gospels of Matthew, Mark and Luke in three columns, with the passages that were similar printed side by side. The other book was full of questions — no answers, just questions. The method was simple; just answer the questions by comparing the three accounts of Jesus' life. The result was captivating — sessions filled with exciting insights into the depth of Jesus' humanity and the genius of his ability to discern God's will.

We live in hurried times. Schedules are full. Each day is packed with activity. There is never enough time to get it all done. Discerning God's will, on the other hand takes time. It requires walks in the park, staring out the window, talking with friends, mulling over alternatives.

"One day when Jesus was praying alone ..." (Luke 9:18). "Jesus took Peter, John and James with him and went up a hill to pray" (Luke 9:28). Jesus often went off to pray. He knew the key to finding God's will. Discernment, in Jesus' day, meant clearing the schedule and putting tasks on hold. It meant making space in one's life for God's voice to be heard. Discernment requires the same discipline today. It involves the ability to put the busyness of life on hold in order to give priority to discerning God's will.

As with the other gifts, discernment is an ability all of us possess to some extent. Discernment as a gift, however, points to a special sensitivity. As a gift it includes a unique patience to walk around issues until the way ahead is clear. It is the gift of the Seer to "see" what others do not notice, to detect needs that generally go undetected, to see past the camouflage of our commercially cluttered lives to the calm flow of God's spirit moving the world in a new and renewing direction.

Spirituality

The gift of spirituality is the ability to sense God's presence in others, in nature, in words and art, and to share that presence with others.

We cherish Jan Richardson's book *In Wisdom's Path*. She has subtitled it, "Discovering the sacred in every season." It is one of those books you can open to any page and find yourself in the presence of God. If her art and the words don't take you on a journey, her poetry will.

It was the gift of spirituality that allowed Elisabeth Barrett Browning to write:

> Earth's crammed with heaven,
> And every common bush afire with God;
> But only he who sees takes off his shoes—
> The rest sit round it and pluck blackberries.
> Book VII, line 820

Not that picking blackberries is bad. It's that spirituality is good.

Being sensitive to the presence of God is one thing. Being able to spark an awareness of God in others is a deeper aspect of spirituality as a gift. Those with the gift of spirituality invite us to stop and experience the wonder of the world for ourselves. It is what Barb Meyer did for us at the conclusion of our course on science and religion:

> All that is beautiful — the spiralling galaxies of the universe; the glory of a morning sunrise; the shades of red, black, yellow and white of the human face; the music of Pachelbel's Canon in D; the wistful smile of the Mona Lisa; the deep-carved lines of an old person's face — is the beauty of God.

Spirituality, with its quest for a personal relationship with the Other behind the universe, offers a way of peace — bypassing the prejudices of established religion in favour of an openness to the wonder of the universe and the presence of a spirit of love within us.

Mentoring

Mentors are those who have skills in an area we want to enter. When Joyce arrived in Edmonton as a single mom, she decided it was time to take her children to Sunday school. A new congregation was starting up in the Mill Woods area where she lived. They were meeting in the music room of a school, some 50 or so people at that time, a small enough group that newcomers were noticed.

The next week the minister Bill Beach came to her house. They had the traditional cup of tea in the living room. Joyce shared her experience of growing up at Avonmore United Church and happened to mention among other things how important participating in the children's choir had been for her.

The next week Joyce got a phone call from Linda Paddon, who was then Chair of the Board at Mill Woods. Bill had told her, she said, that Joyce would be interested in leading a children's choir if they could find her a pianist. Well, she reported, they had found a pianist. Thus began the development not only of a Junior Choir, but also a full band that led the congregation in a "Happy Birthday Jesus" celebration the next Christmas.

Bill then encouraged Joyce to be on a committee, and then to chair a committee. That led to being part of a study group, and then to chairing the Board.

What Bill saw in Joyce was a passion. Nurturing that passion led to deeper insights into Joyce's gifts, and that led to helpful suggestions as to the next step in developing those gifts. Mentoring is about identifying and removing barriers. It includes the ability to discern what resources are really needed, then ensuring they are available.

The first thing Jesus did when he launched his movement was to call twelve individuals into a relationship where he could be their mentor.

We all look for mentors at one time or another in our life. Age is not as much a criteria as experience. When Clair wanted to develop a web site for the Congregational Life Centre, he found the best mentors were his two sons who are in the web site development business.

The relationship between mentor and protégé can be mutually satisfying. For the mentor, it is seeing someone with a passion for their area of expertise soak up everything they can like a sponge. It is watching someone with gifts in an area you think is very important develop their skills and ensure that work goes forward. For the protégé, the one looking to move ahead and develop their abilities, it is an opportunity to get a clear view of the road ahead, to receive that combination of support and prodding that helps with the bumps and keeps one moving.

Mentoring relationships end. It is the wise mentor who can let the learner go when they have absorbed what they need to know. Everybody wins when a mentor-protégé relationship matures into a relationship of two colleagues who continue to be mutually supportive, or a more casual relationship of two friends who have both an experience and a passion for a particular area of life.

Artistic Creativity

Jan Richardson has this to say about people with the gift of artistic creativity:

> Artists risk the vulnerable stance when they open themselves to life. The artist, the crafter of life, gathers in through the senses all of life, the good, the bad, the grit and the grim, the pleasure and the pain, the memories and

the dreams. And, in embracing everything, the artist shatters the limits of
reason, purpose, and duty to risk showing the world what is inside their
heart and our hearts. (37)

The gift of an artist is that he or she lets us see the world in a new way. It is the
development of ways to share that vision that makes the artist so important for the
rest of us. Whether it is poetry or prose or music that paints the picture, art opens
our eyes, expands our mind, frees our spirit, and feeds our soul. That centre,
according to Thomas Moore in his book *Care of the Soul*, is where God's spirit
touches the centre of our being and releases our creative imagination (xiii).

Artistic creativity includes the carpenter who does repairs around the church and the
handy man who fixes a door for a single mom. Someone we know is continuously
making improvements in the nursing home where his wife lives. It is a matter of
attitude more than specific activity. "What are you doing?" Christopher Wren is
reported to have asked the men who were constructing the church he had designed.
"Laying bricks," was one response. "Building a cathedral," was another. That's the
difference. Michelangelo's assistants were removing excess stone from a block of
marble. He was freeing the figure of the David that he knew was inside.

A print of the painting *Starry Night* by Vincent van Gogh hangs in Joyce's hallway.
Galaxies swirl in the night sky, spirals of wonder and light. Did we have telescopes
that could distinguish galaxies back when van Gogh was painting? Whether we did
or not, the pictures gives us a preview of the wonder only now being revealed by the
Hubble and other modern telescopes.

Jesus was an artist with words:

> Blessed are you who are poor, for yours is the kingdom of God.
> Blessed are you who are hungry now, for you will be filled.
>   (Luke 6:20-21)

Can you play the balalaika?" Yuri's brother asked. "Can she play? She's an artist!"
responded her companion. "Then it's a gift," came the assurance.

The Spectrum

These eight gifts together form a spectrum of individual colours. Together they give a picture of how God's love works through individuals to create community and provide a visible demonstration of love in action.

Each of these gifts has a special relationship to the ones on either side. That is why the circles all intersect and overlap.

What the gifts of Leadership and Planning have in common is a vision of where a particular group, individual, or community want to go. It is just that Leadership is more about motivating people to keep their eye on the goal, while Planning provides a roadmap of the turns and twists that constitute the journey.

Communicating and Caring are gifts that compliment each other, because it is through communication that people learn about the caring that is available, and those with a gift for Caring learn where their gift is especially needed.

It is important in Caring to know the spiritual needs of those being cared for. That is where Discernment can be of great assistance. On the other hand, those with the gift of Discernment often see things that are difficult to acknowledge, and as a result have a special need for Care.

Discernment and Spirituality are partners. Discernment functions as the practical side of listening — seeking specific answers to life's questions. Spirituality embodies the creative personal side of that same listening — seeking relationship with that which is beyond.

One aspect of Mentoring is to understand and encourage the spiritual development of another human being. The other side of mentoring is to encourage the growth of creative skills.

> *The quest for true creative growth is as difficult as the quest for spiritual growth, since the two are inextricably intertwined.*
> *Teri Degler,*
> *The Fiery Muse*

Artistic Creativity looks to skilled practitioners and artisans to develop the technical aspects of an art or craft. On the other hand, Artistic Creativity has a real affinity with Leadership. Both gifts look deep inside themselves for insight as to what to create on the one hand, or for a vision of where to lead on the other.

These eight gifts are not restrictive boxes but aptitudes that enhance and flow into one another. That is what we want to convey by portraying these gifts as a spectrum where, just like in a rainbow, the colours flow into each other.

The "Individual Gifts Instrument" in Appendix A is designed to help you identify the gifts that are central for you.

Every human being has some ability in each of the eight gift categories. What makes them special as gifts for an individual is that when we make use of a "gift," we find the process returns more energy to us than it consumes. When we use a gift, what we are doing comes to us as a rush of excitement, energy, and engagement. At the deepest level, we have a sense of being perfectly in tune with the universe and doing exactly what we have been created to do.

3. Using Our Gifts

The place God calls you to is the place where your deep gladness and the world's deep hunger meet.

Frederick Buechner, *Wishful Thinking – A Theological ABC*

We have a Soul

We never doubt the existence of the body with its strength because we feed it, clothe it, and love or hate it every day of our lives. We value our heart both as the organ that keeps our blood circulating and have made it the symbolic home of our emotions. Our mind is where we store and recall information and feelings, as well as the place of conscience and questions.

It seems we have ignored the soul over the last 50 or so years. This is partly because soul is associated with organized religion in the minds of many, and organized religion is getting pretty bad press these days.

For almost 2,000 years, Christianity accepted the concept of soul that originated with Socrates, Plato and the other great minds of Greek philosophy. Plato thought of the soul as an immortal spirit which enters the human mortal body at birth and leaves it at death. It is the soul, Plato taught, that is spiritual and good — the body is mortal, passes, and consequently is far less important.

Theologians in the twentieth century began to question the concept of an immortal soul. A close examination of the Hebrew Scriptures revealed a very different concept from that of Greek philosophy. The Hebrew *nephish* is more like the rudder of a ship, an integral part of us that determines our direction, which steers us ethically. Jesus confirmed the Hebrew commandment that we are to love God with all our heart, with all our soul, with all our strength, and with all our mind" (Luke

10:27 as well as Mark 12). There is no hint that the emotions, mind, and bodily strength are one thing, the soul another. For Jesus and for Hebrew Scriptures, the four are part of the one reality that constitutes a whole human being.

Twentieth century medical science began to observe close links between mental health, spiritual health, and the well being of the whole body. The whole branch we know as psychosomatic medicine came into being.

It is our view that the soul is that place where we feel at peace, where our values connect with our actions, where real joy and sorrow are felt. It is a capacity that is at the very core of who we are as individuals — giving us an identity, making us uniquely human.

There is a growing interest in understanding our soul and how it is nurtured. The number of books available that focus on spirituality continues to grow. One of the top sellers in the late '90s was Thomas Moore's *Care of the Soul*. It was popular because it affirmed the importance of the small things we do every day. The soul, for Moore, is the seat of the creative imagination. By caring for our soul, we nurture the creative imagination that allows us to identify with others, and thus truly care for them.

Using our Gift Nurtures our Soul

We know the decisions we make are right when windows of opportunity open for us. Joyce vividly remembers driving across the James MacDonald Bridge with her son, and feeling the support of the universe because she had just found an excellent day care for her children and a job for herself. Her new life as a single parent had all come together in a matter of days.

Jane, a new entrepreneur, shared with us how several people contacted her the first week she launched her new business, all requesting her services. To her it was a sign that she had made the right decision. She felt useful, accepted, and good.

Offering our gifts for the benefit of others and having that offer accepted is a tremendously nurturing experience. We feel connected with others, with the universe, and if we have a Christian background, with God. Using our gifts for the benefit of others is what we call ministry. We read that when Jesus healed Peter's mother-in-law of a fever she "began to serve them" (Mark 1:31). Jesus had ministered to her. She ministered to Jesus. Life is about ministry. To live is to be in ministry. To be in ministry is to use one's gifts unselfishly, even extravagantly for others. That is the sense in which we use this word.

Using our gifts for the benefit of others is when we stretch ourselves and grow. Most of us know someone who has turned their pain around and used that experience to help others going through a similar challenge. The alcoholic who provides counselling to others is an example, as is the abused woman who supports women in making choices. As a result, victims become victors. While we don't all have painful life experiences to share with others, what we do have are our unique gifts. How we use them is a measure of our growth. When we choose to share our gifts so they benefit others we become richer people ourselves. If we hold them tight, we will be the poorer. Love only grows when you give it away!

You have to decide

Making the decision to explore or apply your gifts can be a very scary one. What if you fail? More frightening, what if you succeed? You may enter into relationships and worlds you never imagined and you aren't sure you can handle. A friend once told Joyce, "Jesus never promised we wouldn't fail." If you are exercising your gift from a place of love and support, neither failure nor success is going to be a deterrent. You will know you are loved just because you took the risk, whether you succeed or not. Of course, it is important to learn from your failures and from your successes, which is what it means to grow.

The main task of our community, our family, and our congregation is to provide the resources we need to support us in living out our ministry. That is what it means for them to be faithful to God's purpose. "One worships this God," in the words of Bishop John Spong, "by loving wastefully, by spreading love frivolously, by giving love away without stopping to count the cost." (72)

The decision to act begins with you. You have to want to explore what your gifts are, where your passions lie, and which community you want to serve. Then you have to develop a plan you can put into action. None of us know what the results will be because God works in mysterious ways. This, however, is certain — you will change. And when one of us changes, so does our world. Scary, isn't it. You do have the power to change the world! The good news is you have company.

Connecting

Take a few minutes, light a candle or find a quiet favourite spot. Then think about the times you have felt most connected with God. Here are a few questions to help:

> Was it when you experienced the love of another?
> Was it as you took a walk in nature?
> Was it when you were working in your garden?
> Was it when you were creating a meal for others?
> Was it when you visited with a friend?
> Was it when you wrote something for another?
> Was it when you experienced music?

Write a prayer that says "thank you" for those times when you have recently felt truly connected, to yourself — to your body, your mind, your heart or your soul — and to God.

4. Channelling Your Passion

Every person in the world has a purpose for being here — a calling. The work of your life is to discover that purpose and get on with the business of living it out. ... There's an old gospel song with a refrain I love: *I've got fire, fire, fire shut up in my bones.* Passion is the log that keeps the fire of purpose blazing. Your work now is to find that fire and rekindle it—and then to let it burn.   - Oprah Winfrey, *O, The Oprah Magazine*

How do we know when we have reached that place where we are doing what God wants us to do? The answer consists of one word — passion. We know we are really connected with the Spirit when our passion is released.

Some have a passion for working directly with people — whether individuals, small groups, or large gatherings. Others are passionate about actualizing their gifts through assembling and sharing information. Still others are passionate about using a particular skill through which they can best exercise their gift or gifts.

When we become passionate, we find that our energy is increased and renewed. It is a sign that we are on the right track — on God's track — when we are receiving more energy from what we are doing than we are expending. Not that we don't get tired, exhausted even, but we emerge from an activity profoundly motivated and with a deep sense of peace.

Exploring your passion is a journey of discovery and honesty, but like any journey, it is relatively easy to get distracted or branch off in a completely wrong direction. When we talk about passion, we do not mean an addiction or an obsession. An addiction is when a drug or a chemical commands your attention. An obsession is when an activity commands your attention. These are both emotions fuelled by a desire to receive. Passion, true passion, is an emotion fuelled by a desire to give, to further the welfare of others, to better oneself in order to make a greater contribution in ones field of endeavour.

Sir Martin Gilbert is a passionate historian. He has written more than 70 books, all carefully researched and documented. A reviewer of his latest volume on victims of the holocaust describes his writing:

> Gilbert's great achievement is not the quantity of his writing; it is the quality. He has the unique ability of being able to break down the huge panorama of human history into small individual pieces of human experience that are readily understandable to his readers. ***His great passion*** [emphasis ours] is to make the facts of important events clear to his audience. He shuns analysis for descriptive material. He prefers his readers to think for themselves and to come to their own judgments. (Abella)

This is what we mean by passion. It is the drive to simplify the complex so that others can understand. It is the desire to think deeply about a subject, to blaze trails that others can follow. It is setting an example that motivates others to develop their own ability to pioneer.

With something as deeply human and as emotionally complex as passion, it is relatively easy to get off track. For that reason, it is helpful to have people who really know you to check things with. It could be a friend, a colleague, or a small group of people that you meet with regularly. It never hurts to check your thinking out with others, and it can be incredibly beneficial.

Following the Passion Trail

What we know about human beings is that we are all different and we do things for many different reasons. Take putting a jigsaw puzzle together for example. Some people want to feel the sense of accomplishment that comes from completing a task. Others like the challenge of fitting the pieces together. For others, it not so much doing the puzzle as the time of rich social and intellectual interaction that they enjoy. Then there are some people who just can't stand jigsaw puzzles.

Clair has a passion for exploring the unknown, putting puzzles together, teaching those with inquiring minds, learning and exploring new theories and universes, and seeing new possibilities — just to name a few. When you match a passion of exploring the unknown with Clair's gifts for leadership and planning, you know you have someone who is going to continue to explore uncharted territory, someone who is not afraid to lead in new directions. Matching gifts and areas of passion points in the direction of certain ministries, and away from others. You would not want to put Clair in a maintenance mode ministry. He would be trying something new every day. He might well be the person to get a new congregation off the ground, to launch a new ministry, to help congregations find new ways of being effective.

People … Information … Skills … Which Will it Be?

Are you someone who works best with people — coaching, mediating to resolve conflict, helping and supporting others? Is your passion visiting with the elderly, providing counselling for those who are troubled, nursing the unhealthy, coaching learners? People who have passions in these areas are those who work in the *people* area.

Do you find that you work best with data or knowledge? Can you read, research and then synthesize information? Do you then deliver an exceptional paper or talk, or do you prefer to do the background work for someone else to use? This indicates you prefer the *information* area.

Are you an artist, musician, builder, or a great cook who can take an idea and develop it into something to share? If your passion is to build on a skill that you have, then you work in the *skill* area.

Each of us is created differently. There will never be another you in history, regardless of what scientists do with cloning technology. God calls us to be the best we can be. This happens when we are serving in areas where we have special gifts.

Too often congregations try to fit a square peg into a round hole. How many people who have a special gift for providing care to others are pressured into an administration position because someone is needed to chair a committee? Have you ever accepted a position for which you had little enthusiasm because "no one else will do it?" If no one volunteers, perhaps that is a message from God that the particular role is not really needed. This approach does not honour the gifts of people, and usually results in burnout or frustration because the work drains energy and does not give satisfaction.

One of the best tests of whether you should say yes or no to a task is to ask yourself, "Does this activity energize me, provide a sense of peace, leave me feeling truly connected to God?" If you can't answer yes, say no.

Some people prefer working with People, others with Information, yet others receive the most satisfaction in utilizing the Skills they possess. When we refer to a primary *Area*, it is the preference for working with people, information or skills that we are exploring.

By *Channels*, we mean the physical setting or means you prefer to use when exercising your gifts. A dedicated teacher may prefer a classroom, the carpenter a woodworking shop. A particular channel can be the setting for a variety of *Activities* — guiding, listening, teaching, etc.

Let's take a closer look at the three primary areas for investing your passion — people, information and skills. Of course we makes use of all three. The question is: which is the primary focus.

People

Those who find their passion best released in dealing directly with people might be nurses, coaches, teachers, mediators, or consultants. If you have a passion for working with people, either one-on-one or in groups, then you just may be a "people person." Most of us enjoy the opportunity to be with people, but some of us have a special talent for being present to individuals and their needs — whether we are having coffee together or exploring an intense problem.

Those with a passion for teaching cherish the relationships that develop in a sharing situation. What students need to learn today is not so much a mass of information about things. The Internet, educational television and an abundance of skilfully crafted books give almost everyone access to a world of data. What people need are ways to find the particular information they need and the overarching concepts that help them make sense of that information. People don't need answers so much as help identifying the questions they need to ask. A people person is someone who helps others to identify their questions.

Workshops are another channel where reaching out to people takes place. Workshops provide the setting for a process that allows people to get to know one another, exchange ideas, and develop a context for informed decision-making.

Another channel for relating to others is the visit. There is an art to visiting. The truly caring visitor moves from exchange at the surface level to deeper sharing of thoughts and perspectives. A visit usually opens with a time of checking in, finding out what has happened since the last encounter. In the next stage it becomes more focused, dealing with a particular topic, a given task, or just getting to know one aspect of each other in more detail. A visit can then move to a deeper level of sharing what has been happening in one's life, at church, with those you love, at work. Then comes the leave taking, a time for real listening. When Clair was visiting members of his congregation, he would always give a five minute warning that he was going to have to leave. That was often a time when something that was troubling finally came out. (Saunders & Woodbury 60)

Within each channel are opportunities for any number of activities. The only limit is the human imagination. Life can be a rich feast of mutually fulfilling interaction. For some, however, it can be a confusing and bewildering place with too many choices to comprehend. The Prisms process is a guide to help individuals navigate the many possibilities and find the path that best utilizes their gifts and is truly satisfying.

Information

Some of us work best with information. We like to research ideas, analyze findings, and file the results so they are accessible. We think of computer programmers as people who work with information, but we should include teachers, speakers, accountants, and managers. So are those of us who love to read, research and discuss some new question or topic.

Working with information is about discovering something new that we may then share with others. Computers, books, articles, interviews, meetings or casual conversation help. These are the channels we can use to share information with others. Many people who work with information keep a journal to record their insights and private reflections. Those with a passion for journaling find it is an excellent way to capture insights for future use. Many of the ideas in this book were first jotted down on napkins in restaurants or on scraps of paper at three in the morning. For the information person, ideas are a commodity of extreme value.

Skills

Are you an artist, musician, builder, a great cook, or perhaps someone who can take an idea, a set of instructions, or a sheet of music, and make it truly live? Do you have a real talent and a passion for putting the pieces of a puzzle together? If so, your primary area for using your gifts may be through exercising a particular skill.

Skills come in thousands of varieties. The way we use those skills include the visual arts, crafts, the music that enriches our lives, the many manual trades practiced by those who construct our buildings and the furnishings that go in them.

Identifying Your Passions

There is a worksheet in Appendix B "Identifying Your Passions" that you can use to get a better grasp of the Area where your passions lie — whether primarily around working with people, gathering information, or using specific skills.

The process makes use of a principle: where you found yourself being passionate in the past is the best indicator of future activities that will release your energy. Where you felt you were living God's call in the past is a compass pointing to effective ministry possibilities for the future.

As you go through the process, do it prayerfully. Find a comfortable place, prop your favourite picture up in front of you or light a candle or put on some music — and listen for the Spirit. Don't be in a hurry and don't be modest. The exercise asks you to:

1. List all your accomplishments. The list should include things you have done in all aspects of your life – work, parenting, volunteering, church, family, etc.

2. Mark the accomplishments you enjoyed most with a star or check mark (√).

3. Identify what it was about each checked accomplishment that made it something you enjoyed or felt good about. Did you feel passionate about

the work or the result? What threads run through your list of accomplishments?

4.   Ask yourself whether it was the information you worked with, the people who were involved, or a special skill that gave you satisfaction in each case. Look down that list. In general, do you most prefer to work with information, people, or skills?

No one works in one area all of the time, and often it takes a blend to produce results. Understanding where your heart lies will help you identify the place where you can be most effective.

When Joyce did this, she found the accomplishments she enjoyed most included teaching people how to do research, delivering workshops to explore goals, mentoring people to understand they have the skills to succeed, and reading to gain new concepts. It all comes down to being passionate about walking with people as they work to make their dreams a reality and their aspirations come true.

As you discover areas that release your passion, please don't see them as boxes that will confine your identity — rather see them as windows you can look through to see new possibilities for yourself.

> The vitality of God be mine this day
> the vitality of the God of life.
> The passion of Christ be mine this day
> the passion of the Christ of love.
> The wakefulness of the Spirit be mine this day
> the wakefulness of the Spirit of justice.
> That vitality and passion and wakefulness of God be mine
> that I might be fully alive this day.
>   J. Philip Newell, *Celtic Benediction.* (53)

5. Companions on the Journey

> Of all living creatures, only humans have the power to shape their own character, to choose between honourable and dishonourable behaviour, to tell the truth or deceive, to exploit or respect others, to work hard or slack off.   Walton, Clarence, *The Moral Manager*

Human beings are fascinating. Did you ever sit at a sidewalk café just watching the people walk by? The varieties are endless — the way we walk, the way we dress, the mood we wear on our face or signal with our stance. The human race is a never ending kaleidoscope of communication.

Added to the fascination is the possibility of a relationship developing with each new person that we meet. The new face may turn out to be a kindred spirit who enriches our life deeply. The very possibility can bring an atmosphere of excitement and wonder to every encounter.

We human beings have some characteristics that are unique — the power to decide, to choose to be or not to be this or that or the other. It is not only who we are that makes us so interesting as individuals, but what we can become.

It is no wonder we are so fascinated with our fellow human beings and energized through working with them — whether directly, or indirectly through the information we gather or the skills we develop. The endless possibilities presented by our fellow humans does present us with a potential problem — decisional meltdown. It is the same situation that confronts a teenager today trying to decide on a career. The list of specializations and sub-sub-occupations is endless. Where to begin? What to do with one's life?

What we need is a way to narrow down just where and how and who it is we want to relate to using the gifts we have been given. Who do we want to be in ministry with? Who will be our companions on the journey. The word *companion* has a long history. *Com-pané* means "with bread." Companions are those with whom you eat bread. They are the ones we minister to and who minister to us on the journey of life.

There are numerous possibilities for "companions on the journey." You need companions who encourage you to release your passion. Without passion, life becomes plodding drudgery. With passion, life becomes a magical mystery tour. Without passion, you will give far more to each day than you receive. When you are travelling through life with those for whom you have passion, doing work which brings out your passion, you will gain energy with each step.

There are criteria other than passion that people use to identify where their life energy needs to be spent — but they offer much less in the way of fulfillment. One of those is charity — feeling sorry for others and wanting to help the "less fortunate." Charity is all well and good. A lot of good work is done by charitable organizations. In ministry, however, we want to go beyond good intentions. We want to identify with others to the point where we see our destiny wrapped up with theirs.

> *If you have come to help me, you are wasting your time. But if you have come because your liberation is bound up with mine, then let us work together.*
>
> *Lila Watson*
> *Australian Aboriginal leader*

Another criteria used all too often is guilt. Do you know couples who have stayed together "for the sake of the children," but whose constant fighting and bickering have had a worse effect than if they had separated? The caregiver who acts out of guilt can end up giving more death than life, if not to the one cared for, then to him or her self. Guilt only works with those who already feel too guilty. Ministry is about getting rid of guilt, not adding to it.

Passion is where we begin, then we look at who we identify with. We identify with people who are like us because we know and understand what they are dealing with. We identify with people who are experiencing what we have experienced because we know what they are going through. Identification, however, is not the whole story. The Christian call to ministry goes beyond loving those with whom we identify, to loving those we do not understand, loving those who are not like us, those whose experiences we have not shared and cannot share. We can do that because, as Christians, we recognize they are loved by God as are we.

This is just another way of saying our welfare is bound up with the welfare of everyone on the globe. There are people we do not like. There are people we despise. There are destructive people whose actions have to be condemned and their freedom to harm others taken away. But if there are any of these we do not love, any we do not honour as unique individuals with possibilities for change and new life, we ourselves are diminished and are acting in a way that is less than human. Spiritual maturity means knowing with our heart that love is at the core of the universe, feeling a love for everything in creation emanating from the depths of our being.

Vaclav Havel, poet and former President of Czechoslovakia, was shaped by that experience while imprisoned. Mary Doria Russell describes the experience in her fictional book, *The Sparrow:*

> There are times . . . when we are in the midst of life — moments of confrontation with birth or death, or moments of beauty when nature or love is fully revealed, or moments of terrible loneliness — times when a holy and awesome awareness comes upon us. It may come as deep inner stillness or as a result of overflowing emotion. It may seem to come from beyond us, without any provocation, or from within us, evoked by music or by a sleeping child. If we open our hearts at such moments, creation reveals itself to us in all its unity and fullness.... When my people search for a name to give to the truth we feel at those moments, we call it God, and when we capture that understanding in timeless poetry, we call it praying. (390)

All this being said, there are natural affinities that we do well to follow. It is always wise to begin where our strengths lie. We are going to look at group size, age cohorts, and gender. With respect to each of these, the challenge is to identify who we are best able to work with as co-travellers on the journey of life. We will add three other categories that deal more specifically with relationships — those who need healing, conflict situations, and power alignments.

Group Size

Some of us prefer to work with individuals. We appreciate an opportunity to get to know another person and explore areas that we have in common. We can often relate in a deeper way with an individual than we can with people in a group situation. With an individual, dialogue can create a two way street where inner thoughts are brought into the open. We can alternate between being a creative listener and a dialogue partner.

Others find that more of their passion is released in a small group. We define a small group as one containing twelve persons or less. There are particular dynamics associated with a small group that make this relationship unique. It is the size of group where we can not only relate to each person, but be aware of the relationship between each member of the group and each of the other members. It is a size where we can establish a covenant of confidentiality and feel confident that what we say in the group stays in the group. This combination of knowing the group and having confidence in its confidentiality allows for safe sharing and consequently growth at a deep and spiritual level. Jesus chose twelve disciples for a reason. It is the group size with the greatest potential for personal support and spiritual development.

In the family size group, up to fifty persons, people know one another well and are there for each other when needed. It is the size of a typical extended family, and has similar characteristics.

The majority of congregations are what we call a Fellowship Group with a maximum of 150 individuals. This is the size that relates to a single leader. They may not know the names of everyone in the group, but feel a common bond in their ability to relate to that leader and espouse a common vision and goals. Some people function very naturally as a leader in this size group. It is the typical congregation where the pastor knows everyone, connects regularly with each person in the group, and develops a deep sense of personal rapport with the entire group.

Larger assemblies tend to be made up of numbers of small groups, family groups and fellowship groups. An assembly of groups requires leadership that embodies a vision that the groups hold in common. That leadership can be charismatic, projecting a personality based on the group's vision that attracts emotional loyalty. On the other hand, it can be administrative, ensuring that the vision and mission are part and parcel of the decision making process.

Take a moment to think about which size group where you receive most of your support. The size where you are most comfortable playing a leadership role.

Age Cohorts

We may have a passion to exercise our gifts through working with a particular age group. Some of us relate best to children. Others have the energy and vocabulary to relate to teens. Yet others feel most at home with young adults, people in midlife, or seniors. It has something to do, of course with our own age. On the other hand, most of us know at least one fifty year old who exhibits many of the characteristics of a teenager and relates well to that age group.

Gender

Our preferences may be gender-focused. Some of us are most at home working with a mixed group of men and women, or girls and boys. Others feel more comfortable working with their own gender. Some feel most comfortable working with the opposite gender. Sometimes, where one works comfortably is very dependent on the topic being discussed. Whatever your choice may be, be aware of where it is you feel most comfortable and relate with the most effectiveness.

Healing and Problem Solving

Some of us relate best to healthy situations — relationships that are doing well and just want to relate better, congregations that are thriving and want to be even more effective.

There are others, and we are grateful for them, who work with the sick. They are the doctors and the nurses, the hospital and home care visitors, who make such a difference in people's lives at a time of illness and strain. There is an intense satisfaction in helping someone back to health.

Organizations and individuals confront problems or find themselves in the middle of a conflict on a regular basis. Problem solving brings with it the satisfaction of putting the pieces of a puzzle together. Dealing with conflict leads to the satisfaction of seeing relationships healed, or dissolved in a way that the parties can set about living healthy independent lives.

Power

Power makes some people very nervous. For others, it is the elixir of life. There is nothing intrinsically bad about power, nor intrinsically good either for that matter. Power is the ability to control the resources around us, whether human or material. We can do that for good, or for ill.

Some Christians feel most comfortable and a real sense of calling working with those who are powerless in order to help them attain the power they need to control their own destiny. Others feel called to work with those in power, in order to encourage the use of that power for the good of others.

Like Jesus, one who was able to do both was Mahatma Ghandi. Perhaps that is what makes him such a saint in our eyes. He identified with the most powerless in India, the untouchables and the village peasants who eked out a subsistence living from the soil. He called upon the ruling English class to give up their power for the sake of a new India. He challenged Hindu and Moslem leaders alike to use their power to create a non-violent society where people could live and work together in harmony.

The variety in the human race is incredible. When doing ministry, it is a matter of working with those with whom we can identify. We know when we are with the right people, the right situation, when we find our passion released, our caring deepened, our commitment strengthened and our energy flowing effortlessly and freely.

Appendix C "Companions on the Journey" provides a way to identify the size of groups you prefer and type of situations where you find your energy is released and caring deepened.

6. Looking at Community

Each of us is a member of a number of communities. There may be one group of people that we work with and completely different folks we work out with on the trail or at the gym. Our hobbies may lead us to associate with yet others, and of course, our extended family is a community with whom we may be in contact continually or just once in a while.

As we mature, our communities change. Our journey through life may lead us into a relationship, followed by parenting, and then a time of being single again or living the freedom of an empty-nest couple. Adult children may move back home, bringing grandchildren with them. We change careers as new opportunities arise. We will likely move from one neighbourhood to another, if not one continent to another, in the course of our life. Many communities come and go through the years; some involve friendships and relationships that continue through our whole life.

Being responsive to the message of the Good News requires that we share our gifts and passions with those who are members of our various communities. It is not just about what we do within the walls of the church that is important. We are normally with our church community only a few hours a week. Far more important is how we live our lives the rest of the time. A father of teens told us one day that his current ministry was to be with his sons at the hockey rink on Sunday morning. We agreed with his thinking, and would like to challenge some of those in congregations who believe that everything has to be set aside so people can attend worship on Sunday.

For that father, the hockey community was where he wanted to make a difference, especially for his son. When we look at where we can use a particular gift, the communities that we are already part of should be the first place to consider. The sports club that you belong to may need someone with a gift for helping plan the next season. In the process you can help build the means into that plan for helping those who might otherwise be left out. The office where you work may need your gift of mentoring to challenge one or two of the newer people to reach their full potential. Underneath, you know that is what God wants us all to do — be the best we can and reach our full potential wherever we are. The family of which you are a part may need your gift of spirituality to ensure the candles are lit for Sunday dinner and the children are tucked into bed with a prayer.

Some of us may want to look beyond to communities that are new for us, places with expanded opportunities for using a gift we want to use and develop. A friend, recently retired from a job related to water resources, volunteered to go to Ethiopia to help farmers develop wells for irrigation. A fish farmer went off to work with the United Nations Food and Agricultural Agency. He ended up helping people in the Philippines and a number of other countries develop their own fish farms to add badly needed protein to their diets. It may be volunteering for service at the men's shelter in your own inner city community, putting a passion for caring into talking to the men, or a gift of artistic creativity in developing murals to speak of hope to any who pass by.

A truly Christian community is very different from much of the world around. As an example, the saying certainly applies to the secular community that "bad news travels fast." Our newspapers are a perfect example — the bad news splashed across the front page with the good news buried on page nine. The early church saw its mandate to "go into all the world," sharing the *good news* that God is love and that our task is to love our neighbour with that same love. In a truly Christ-like community, it is the good news that travels fast.

We have identified eleven types of communities: the Arts, Church, Home, Extended Family, Friends, Neighbourhood, Athletics, Recreation, School, Work, and the World. We invite you to review them, and as you do, ask how your gifts might be put to use in one or more of them.

The Arts: There are many arts-related communities that centre on music, art, dance, or drama. The writing community itself is composed of those whose skill tends toward adult fiction, young adult fiction, poetry, non-fiction — the list of categories is quite long. The arts are about creating, and about performing — two very different perspectives. The question here is not so much whether we are a gifted artist, but whether there is an arts organization or group who need our particular gifts, whether they be organizing a fund raising drive or welcoming people to an arts event.

Church: For most people, church means the local congregation to which they belong. Some will be involved in denominational structures at a local, regional or national level. Your connection with a church will change over time. Today congregations specialize in meeting particular needs. The days when a congregation was able to be "all things to all people" are past, if that ever was a reality. Choosing a congregation means looking for one that can make use of your particular gifts and answer your particular needs.

Home: Most people think of the nuclear family of father, mother and two children as normal. That situation is less and less the case with the reality being that there are more and more blended families and single parent families. Under this category of "home" we include any group of people who have decided to live together. A college dormitory is home for many students. Volunteers living in group homes of the L'Arche community are sharing an inspiring ministry with the mentally challenged. There is a saying, "home is where the heart is." Putting the heart into wherever we live is a ministry of using our gifts to create a true home environment.

Extended Family: At one point it became difficult to hold extended families together as adult offspring found work that took them across the continent if not around the world. Improvements in air travel and increased retirement incomes have worked to increase contact and bring extended families much closer. Today it is not uncommon for grandparents to jet half way across the continent to care for grandchildren while parents take a holiday.

Friends: Some people are friends for life, and some friendships are more like ships that pass in the night. Regardless, these relationships provide opportunities for mutual support and growth.

Neighbourhood: The geographic neighbourhood has become less and less a community where we know and relate in a meaningful way to others. We may know the people who live either side or us, but few others as we commute to work and cocoon at home. For some of us, however, our geographic neighbours have become friends and members of a true community of mutual caring.

Athletics: You may participate or be a spectator in some form of sports or athletics. Jogging with a friend can be a time for intimate sharing. Slow-pitch softball is gaining popularity as a way to spend a summer evening with friends. Golf, says Scott Peck, is a spiritual exercise that teaches true humility — and provides an opportunity for making business contacts or renewing relationships.

Recreation: Building model trains, an evening of bridge, going to a movie with a friend, taking a long walk with a companion, playing with grandchildren — all are opportunities to use our gifts in that special way that makes a difference for others.

School: This is a community that changes as you and your children move through the education system.

Work: You may spend a large portion of your time at a place of work. If your abilities are being well used, you should have many opportunities to use your gifts. Some of us think that Christian ministry means talking about God or encouraging people to come to church. Jesus' ministry, however, was not about getting people to attend synagogue more often. "Love your neighbour as yourself," was his advice. If you examine the parables, they are all about helping others, being fair in your dealings, putting first things first, and sharing with those who are less fortunate. There are numerous opportunities for that kind of ministry in the workplace.

The World: Many of us support organizations that reach out around the world. For some that support comes in the form of financial assistance, but for others, it is a matter of travelling to another country and offering one's services. A number of volunteer and semi-professional agencies offer opportunities for those who feel a call in this direction.

You may wish to add other categories of community to these eleven. For each of us, it is a matter of identifying the communities where we can use our gifts, and as a result make a meaningful contribution to the welfare of the people there. Appendix D "Community Opportunities" contains a work sheet that can help with that task.

7. Exploring your Personal Gifts

One of the ongoing wonders of our world is that it is made up of millions of unique individuals each with different gifts and passions. When we use those gifts as individuals we can make a difference in the lives of those around us. When we combine our gifts with those of others, can change the world. It is a matter of recognizing our gifts and going for it.

If you are reviewing your gifts on your own, it is important to take the time to do some pondering where they are leading you.

Appendix E "Your Personal Prism" provides a page where you can circle all the categories that apply to you and get an overall picture of your preferences. To pull it all together you are asked to write a paragraph describing yourself, based on the information you have discerned so far. It should include:

- Your top two or three gifts as revealed by the Spiritual Gifts Instrument.
- The Area in which you prefer to work, whether with People, Information or Skills.
- What makes accomplishments special for you?
- The Channels you prefer.
- The Activities in which you experience the most passion.
- The Companions on the Journey with whom you feel most energized.
- The communities where you currently have the greatest opportunities to use your gifts.

Fasten that paragraph or summary page on your wall, beside the mirror, over your desk, or inside your daily calendar — someplace where it will keep you thinking. Take some time to sit on a rock by the water, or find a comfortable chair and stare off into space. The questions you will want to ponder are these: "What is this information about myself saying? What is God calling me to do?"

A third way to explore what the Prisms process is saying to you is to use the Prisms Wheel. When you have finished colouring your key Gifts, writing in your preferred Channels, colouring your Companions on the Journey (favourite group sizes) and writing in the Communities you relate to, punch the centre holes and assemble the circles using the brass pin. Then spin the wheel to reveal as many combinations as possible. Play with it. Carry it with you, and if you have some spare moments, ask what it is telling you. It is in taking the time to listen for God's message that the real work of discernment takes place.

When you have completed your instruments, we encourage you to share the results with a small group who can help you understand the possibilities for you. It might be one or two friends, or a group of six or so members of an organization you belong to. (If there are more than six persons, it will become difficult to include everyone unless the members of the group know each other well.) Probably four people you trust is the ideal size for this type of consultation.

Give your friends a run-down of what your Prism has told you so far:

- What has the process confirmed for me.
- What surprised me about the results or the process.
- Where I think the results are dead on.
- Where I think the results are off base.
- Where I have questions, having gone through this process.

After sharing your reaction and questions, the others in your group should share their perceptions of what your Prism is saying to you.

When you are alone — take all of this information, light a candle or put on some meditative music or find a favourite spot where you can celebrate the journey, and begin the process of discerning what, if anything, you want to do with your new knowledge. This is where long walks, times of reflection, journaling, and prayer help you get in touch with the God in you and how you are being called to live out your life.

Each of us has a mental picture of who we are. The clearer the picture, the stronger our sense of identity — and in many ways that is a good thing. When we are called upon to change, however, that call can challenge our self-image. We may feel under attack, and the natural reaction to that is to react defensively with anger or withdrawal. If you feel this process is calling you to use your gifts in a new say, it will take courage to look at the new you that could emerge and say yes to giving it a try.

Jesus spent time blessing children who were brought to him. We read that he used one such occasion to remind his followers, "Whoever does not receive God's new community as a little child will never enter it" (Luke 18:17). You have seen children playing dress-up, a girl in her mother's party dress, a boy clomping around in an old pair of his father's shoes. They are trying out different roles to see if they fit. That's what it takes to move into the future for children, and it's the attitude we need as individuals if we are to expand our mental map of who we are and move into the future.

By trying out a role, that does not mean you have to adopt it forever. Like the children at play, you can try something on, keep it if it fits, or change to something else if that seems better.

One more word — don't be in a hurry to rush the process. For some, a door will open right away. Others will find they are at the beginning of a much longer journey. How will the insight come? Some people will have an epiphany — a sudden moment of understanding when the road ahead becomes clear. For others, the answer may come more obliquely — through the remark of a friend, a phone call that reveals an opportunity, or a growing consciousness of a way to meet someone's need. Whatever way an avenue opens for you, create a plan and take action to begin to live out that call.

8. Working with Groups

This resource can also be used with small or larger groups. When we work together in groups, we combine resources and insights, bouncing ideas off one another, encouraging one another, sometimes daring one another to follow our dream.

A Small Group

Most of us belong to several small groups. Those we live with are one — our family, our significant other, our roommate. Many serve on a church committee. Those who are fortunate are members of a small group who meet intentionally to learn together and care for each other. It could be a temporary gathering specifically called together for a Prisms event. Whatever the intent, combining your individual Prisms into a corporate Prism reflecting the nature of the group can have real benefits.

When the individuals in a group have completed their Prism you can build a group picture by creating a large circle that identifies gifts common to members of the group. There are a number of benefits to doing this. Understanding the individual gifts of group members can provide insight into the focus of the group's activities. If the group has a clear picture of what it wants to do, a knowledge of individual gifts can be the basis for assigning various roles in the project.

Be clear about the purpose of sharing in a small group — whether it is to help individuals identify ministries that suit their gifts, or to identify a ministry which the group might like to undertake in common. In either case, it is important to have a process that provides an opportunity to share and get feedback individually, as well as time for open group discussion.

Make sure that everyone participating is passionate about being there. If they are there because they think they need to be, rather than because they want to be, they may well take more energy away from the group process than they contribute. Both energy and commitment are important. We don't know everything about God, but we do know it is hard for God to get through to those who are lethargic or reticent.

Each member should have completed all of the Prism instruments in advance, and come prepared to share. Obtain a copy of the *Prisms Workbook* for each member and distribute them at least a week before your gathering.

Candles can help set the mood, or music, or art, or food — or all of these. One way of using candles is for the group to sit in a circle around a low table containing enough candles for each member. At some point, people share while lighting their candle. A Christ candle lit at the beginning of the session says that you are there to listen, not just talk.

We found boxes of irregular plastic prisms at a Christmas decorations store. They make an excellent symbol for the centre of the table, and one can be given to each person at the conclusion of the time together as a way of taking home a reminder of the group.

You may want to provide special journals or paper and pens for those who need something to write on — so they can record the questions and insights that arise during the session.

An outline of a session that leads a small group through a process of sharing and exploring their individual gifts can be found in Appendix F "Exploring Gifts as a Group."

Large Group

Understanding who we are as a large group can provide insights about ministry, programs, and resources. Knowing the gifts that are present in a congregation, for example, can assist in identifying outreach activities that utilize the strengths of the congregation and ways the congregation can better serve the needs of its members.

Much of the process we have outlined for a small group can apply to a larger gathering. The important thing is for people to have the opportunity to work in small groups at various points in the process in order to give them an opportunity to explore what they have to offer as individuals.

When it comes to getting an overall picture, a Gifts Chart can help. Mount a large circle divided into eight segments, each named after one of the eight gifts, on a piece of corkboard or cardboard. Give everyone an opportunity to insert coloured pins identifying main gifts. The resulting picture will give an indication where the strengths of the community lie. Exploring what that means will provide insights into possible ministries or strong focal points for the group or congregation's life together.

The Gifts Chart can also help you identify the skills you need to have in staff leadership or where you might need to contract for help in specific areas. Where there are gaps in the gifts of a congregation's members, and yet the congregation wants to do a project or provide a service in that area, staff or consultants with those gifts could complement the congregation's abilities and provide leadership.

Action Plan

Whether you use this resource in small groups or with large groups, the challenge is to act on what you learn. There is no perfect action plan, but you have to have a plan if you are going to take action. Having a good idea is not enough. We have seen too many congregations stay with the devil they know rather than go for the good that requires change. The congregation that decides to model its ministry on the gifts of its people rather than the traditions of its denomination faces an uphill struggle.

There have been a number of books written on leading an organization through a change process. The first step is to gather a core of people who are committed to making the needed change. Our Congregational Life newsletter published the story of how Gordon Oaks went about introducing a small group ministry approach in his church (December 2002). Gordon spent a year doing research into small group ministry. Then came trips with lay people to conferences and a year and a half training small group leaders before launching the program. All in all, it was a five-year process. Start small and build is one aspect of introducing change.

The other is getting more energy on side with the new than is committed to the traditional. In layman's language, get more people on your side than they have on theirs. It was the consultant guru Lyle Schaller who pointed out the importance of getting more people on your Board committed to the new than are bound to the traditional. If not, the traditional side will wear down the new with blocking tactics and revert to the old ways at the first opportunity.

Any group that leads change has to embody that change in their own being. That means developing leadership for an approach based on gifts. It means using every opportunity to celebrate gifts — gift banners, bulletin covers that highlight gifts, special Sunday's devoted to lifting up the gifts of different people. When a ministry based on gifts is woven into the fabric of a congregation, there is strength in that congregation.

Not everyone is going to take part in a process, nor must they. It is important in these days of transition to have a foot on both shores, honouring the traditional at the same time as the new is made available. Balancing on one foot is a little risky, and one can only hold the pose so long. Try it yourself if you don't believe us. Balancing on two feet, well apart, is the equivalent of continuing to honour the old while experimenting with the new. A congregation maintains its balance when that happens. You just need a little more weight on the foot that is pointing to the future, because that is the direction you want to move.

The final step is just doing it. The courage to begin is where the real journey starts.

Prisms

Appendix A
Individual Gifts Instrument

As you answer these questions, think as openly as you can of who you are in as many situations as possible — in your home, at work, with friends, at church, engaged in a favourite activity, etc. Answer each as quickly as you can. Trust your intuitions and record your initial responses.

For each of the following statements:

- if you **strongly agree,** or it applies to you **most of the time**, enter   2
- if you **moderately agree,** or it applies to you **some of the time**, enter   1
- If you do not agree, or the statement does not apply to you, enter   0

1   I love dreaming about the possibilities for organizations I am a part of.

2   A clear strategy is what every organization needs.

3   I like speaking to groups of people.

4   Caring for people brings me close to God.

5   I tend to stick with a problem until an answer emerges.

6   I frequently feel close to God.

7   Being a model for the next generation is very important.

8   Music, poetry, art, dance, drama — any one of these can be a window through which I see God.

9   I am energized when I am being creative.

10   Walking with another person is the best way to help them on their journey.

11   I want people to recognize the God in me.

2 – applies most of the time   1 – some of the time   0 – does not apply

12   I find my mind mulling over issues and coming up with possibilities. ☐

13   I enjoy encouraging people when they are discouraged. ☐

14   I believe my presentations really connect with people. ☐

15   If you know where you are going, you have some possibility of getting there. ☐

16   I have read a number of books on leadership and motivation. ☐

17   I enjoy helping groups of people get organized. ☐

18   Taking time to plan helps me to deal with the unforeseen. ☐

19   I communicate by adopting a style that matches the audience. ☐

20   Being with people who are grieving or ill gives me a feeling that I have done some good. ☐

21   I look for at least three alternatives before making a decision. ☐

22   I find God in every one. ☐

23   There is nothing as satisfying as helping someone come to an understanding. ☐

24   I share my love of God through a creative vehicle (like art, writing, poetry, drama, dance, etc.). ☐

25   Creating something unique and new is very exciting. ☐

26   It is important to pass on what I have learned about life. ☐

27   I can feel when God's Spirit is moving in a group. ☐

28   My approach to an issue is to walk around it until I gain an insight. ☐

29   I try to make people feel special. ☐

2 – strongly agree   1 – moderately agree   0 – do not agree

30   People in a group respond when I am speaking.

31   I can recommend a process for finding out what you want to know.

32   Tell me where you want to go, and I'll get you there.

33   I love helping a group reach their goals.

34   A step-by-step plan is helpful for achieving success.

35   Sharing stories from my own experience is a good way to communicate with people.

36   Meeting people is one of my gifts.

37   I get ideas popping into my head at the strangest times.

38   I take time frequently to feed my soul.

39   There is nothing like sharing with someone eager to learn.

40   I am deeply moved by a piece of music or work of art.

41   I have always played an instrument, painted or written stories.

42   Young people are like sponges, just soaking up what they need to know.

43   I experience God in more ways than most people are aware of.

44   I believe God speaks to us through others.

45   I have a knack for remembering names and faces.

46   I come away from doing a presentation feeling energized.

47   I am willing to take charge if it means the task will be done well.

2 – applies most of the time   1 – some of the time   0 – does not apply

48	Looking at the future is scary, but it is also very exciting.	
49	I have a knack for motivating others to reach a goal.	
50	I am skilled at helping groups develop a plan.	
51	I communicate clearly and effectively with others.	
52	I find just being there is an effective way of caring for people.	
53	"What would my spiritual guide (Jesus, God, Buddha, a favourite saint) do in this situation?" is a question I frequently ask.	
54	The spirituality section is one of the places I check out in any bookstore.	
55	I feel I'm really helping people when I challenge them to make their own decisions.	
56	I am keen to develop my artistic skills (art, music, drama, photography, etc.).	
57	I like designing and creating things.	
58	I enjoy providing guidance and support for individuals.	
59	I look for opportunities to talk about spiritual things.	
60	Dealing with an issue involves taking the time to let God's answer emerge.	
61	I am totally present when talking to someone.	
62	When called upon to make a presentation, I work hard to make sure I am prepared.	
63	I am good at facilitating group process.	
64	I can adjust my leadership style to fit the situation.	

2 – strongly agree   1 – moderately agree   0 – do not agree

Scoring

Place your scores for each question in the appropriate box. Note … the box numbers go left to right, then backwards right to left alternately. Total your score for each spiritual gift.

1 →	2	3	4	5	6	7	8
16	15	14	13	12	11	10	9 ←
17	18	19	20	21	22	23	24
32	31	30	29	28	27	26	25
33	34	35	36	37	38	39	40
48	47	46	45	44	43	42	41
49	50	51	52	53	54	55	56
64	63	62	61	60	59	58	57
Leadership	Planning	Communi-cating	Caring	Discernment	Spirituality	Mentoring	Artistic Creativity

On the following pages you will find two ways of visualizing what your scores say about your gifts. Choose the one that feels most appropriate for you.

Your Spiritual Gifts Profile

For each gift, colour the number of rings to equal your score, starting from the centre.

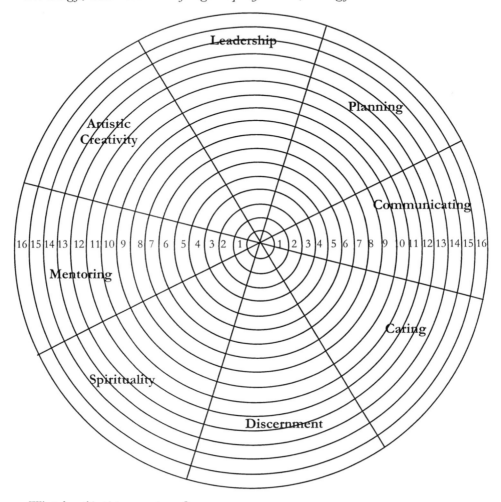

What does this picture say to you?

Here is an alternative way to profile your gifts. Circle the number in each category that reflects your score, then join the circles.

Leadership	Planning	Communi-cating	Caring	Discernment	Spirituality	Mentoring	Artistic Creativity
16	16	16	16	16	16	16	16
15	15	15	15	15	15	15	15
14	14	14	14	14	14	14	14
13	13	13	13	13	13	13	13
12	12	12	12	12	12	12	12
11	11	11	11	11	11	11	11
10	10	10	10	10	10	10	10
9	9	9	9	9	9	9	9
8	8	8	8	8	8	8	8
7	7	7	7	7	7	7	7
6	6	6	6	6	6	6	6
5	5	5	5	5	5	5	5
4	4	4	4	4	4	4	4
3	3	3	3	3	3	3	3
2	2	2	2	2	2	2	2
1	1	1	1	1	1	1	1
0	0	0	0	0	0	0	0

What does this profile say to you?

Below are brief definitions of the gifts and how they can be used in living life fully.

Leadership

Leaders are the vision holders of a community. They have the ability to motivate, inspire, manage, and encourage others. People look to leaders for support and guidance. Sometimes leaders are out front showing the way, at other times they are behind, guiding and supporting. Leaders are listeners who embody a group's core values and perspectives.

How this gift might be shared:

As the vision holder, the leader is the one who is aware of the direction things are moving and set goals for success. Leaders:

❑   Articulate and communicate the vision and goals of the community.
❑   Take responsibility for leading groups (or ensuring a leader is in place).
❑   Manage people and resources effectively.
❑   Take the initiative to ensure that new things are happening.

Planning

A planner helps a group develop the strategy and the tactics that will enable it to move toward its vision. Planning is the ability to develop a process to get the work done.

How this gift might be shared:

❑   Assist groups to develop an action plan with the strategies and tactics required to complete their assigned task.
❑   Organize the people and resources required for specific projects.

❑   Consult with organizations around ways to bring order out of chaos (a tall order, but the opportunities are everywhere).
❑   Ensure the steps are clear for achieving each goal the community sets for itself.

Communicating

Those with the gift of communicating are able to share a message with others and have it received and understood at both the intellectual and emotional levels. Communicators are people who listen until they are clear about the message, and then develop ways to share that information effectively. They know how to make a message memorable. They are storytellers.

How this gift might be shared:

❑   Building bridges between people.
❑   Participating in events as storytellers and readers.
❑   Presenting the pros and cons of a particular situation.
❑   Articulating the vision and mission of the group in ways that capture the imagination.

Caring

Those with a gift for caring are able to develop quick rapport with people. They come across as people you can talk to, share with, have confidence in. Whether visiting the sick or greeting newcomers, they have a way of making people feel that they really matter. Many caregivers are connectors, linking people with the help or services they need.

Care providers are foundational to serving those the community wants to serve. The needs are many, but caring people are those who choose to work where the needs are greatest. They provide care for seniors, for youth, the sick, people in palliative care, or the recently bereaved. They reach out to others not just with physical help, but also with emotional support. They embody empathy.

How this gift might be shared:

- ❑ Ensure newcomers are warmly greeted and create a welcoming atmosphere at meetings and gatherings.
- ❑ Embody what it means to be truly hospitable.
- ❑ Visit people who are going through a period in their life when they need support.
- ❑ Provide a listening ear for those who need someone to talk to.
- ❑ Identify needs in the community, and encourage others to meet those needs.

Discernment

The gift of discernment is an ability to clearly define issues, a creative imagination that can perceive answers, and the patience to stay with an issue until those answers make themselves clear. It includes an ability to research issues and discern the wisdom needed to make effective decisions. Discerners are able to help with decision making and can offer advice in a number of areas. They can apply spiritual truth to inform specific situations.

How this gift might be shared:

- ❑ Identify practical solutions to pressing problems.
- ❑ Help resolve differences of opinion by coming up with creative approaches.
- ❑ Identify the marginalized in a community and their specific needs.
- ❑ Help a congregation or group answer the question, "Is this God's will?"

Spirituality

Spirituality is the gift of a special sensitivity to the movement of the Spirit. People with this gift are aware of the multiple ways that individuals experience God. It is the ability to sense God's presence in others, in nature, in art.

How this gift might be shared:

- ❏ Develop ways of sharing the resources found to be effective in deepening spirituality.
- ❏ Facilitate prayer groups.
- ❏ Act as a spiritual guide or take training as a spiritual director.
- ❏ Advise those responsible for worship on ways to increase the spirituality component.

Mentoring

Mentoring is about facilitating learning by being a companion. These are the teachers and enablers who help people to develop their faith and their gifts. This includes the gift of teaching, because education is walking with people as they journey.

How this gift might be shared:

- ❏ Support for those who are going through a familiar life experience.
- ❏ Institute a mentoring program with the purpose of supporting young people on their journey.
- ❏ Become a teacher who walks the learning journey beside those who wish to learn.
- ❏ Be alert to the potential gifts in people, and develop ways to encourage their development and use.

Artistic Creativity

Music, visual art, the written word, dance and
drama — these are all creative gifts. These gifts
can be used to appeal to people with diverse
learning styles and therefore create a more
inclusive environment. This gift includes
anything from carpentry and creative plumbing
to freeing a masterpiece from marble.

How this gift might be shared:

- ❑   Enhance the worship experience with your art.
- ❑   Use art to engage more of the senses in worship.
- ❑   Set a tone in which people see even simple repairs as a creative expression.
- ❑   Design room decor that sets an ambiance of spirituality.
- ❑   Help people explore spiritual truth or life issues through image and metaphor.
- ❑   Provide an art form that embodies a goal or future direction.
- ❑   Encourage creative thinking through play.

Appendix B
Identifying Your Passions

The purpose of this second exercise is to enable you to identify the particular Areas, Channels and Activities where you have the most passion for exercising your key gifts.

Some people prefer working with People, others with Information, yet others receive the most satisfaction in utilizing the Skills they possess. When we refer to your primary *Area*, it is your preference for people, information or skills that we are exploring.

By *Channels*, we mean the physical setting or means you prefer to use when exercising your gifts. A dedicated teacher may prefer a classroom, the carpenter a woodworking shop.

A particular channel can be the setting for a variety of *Activities* — guiding, listening, teaching, etc.

Find a comfortable place where you can relax, close your eyes, and dream. If you would like, light a candle or turn on some music.

This exercise has two parts:
- o   Use the Accomplishments section to identify whether you prefer to work in the Area of people, information or skills.
- o   Use the three pages that follow to identify the Channels and Activities that fit for you, with special attention to the page for your primary Area.

Accomplishments

1. Using the worksheet on the next page, list the accomplishments that stand out for you during your lifetime. Include accomplishments that have to do with:
    - work
    - parenting
    - extended family
    - church
    - friends

2. Mark the accomplishments you enjoyed most with a star(☆) or check (✓).

3. In the third column, try to identify what it was about the accomplishment that made it something you enjoyed or felt good about. Did you feel passionate about the work or the result?

4. In the fourth column, name the major Area of this passion, whether People, Information or Skills.

PS: Don't think of these as boxes that confine your identity — rather see them as windows you can look through to expand your range of possibilities.

Step 1. Name Accomplishments	2. √	Step 3. What Made it Special?	Step 4. Primary Area: People, Information or Skills?

Make a note as to whether your primary Area is as a People, Information or Skills person:

_____

The next three pages give you an opportunity to identify Channels and Activities that fit for you. Give special attention to the page that contains your primary Area.

Working with People

1. Circle Channels that fit for you, ones you have used in the past and see yourself continuing to use in the future. If your favourite is not here, write it in.

2. Circle the words that best correspond to Activities where you have experienced yourself having passion in the past. If your favourite activity is not here, write it in.

Channels	Activities
dialogue	coaching
classroom	representing
workshops	consulting
visits	motivating
group activities	guiding
	managing
	initiating
	referring
	listening
	helping
	resolving conflict
	serving
	sharing an experience
	teaching

3. Now, define the words you have circled or written in with a sentence.

Working with Information

1. Circle Channels that fit for you, ones you have used in the past and see yourself continuing to use in the future. If your favourite is not here, write it in.

2. Circle the words that best correspond to Activities where you have experienced yourself having passion in the past. If your favourite activity is not here, write it in.

Channels	Activities
computers	gathering
books	gaining knowledge
interviews	analyzing
articles	adapting
classroom	senses
journaling	implementing
	record keeping
	problem solving
	managing
	synthesizing

3. Now, define the words you have circled or written in with a sentence.

Working with Skills

1. Circle Channels that fit for you, ones you have used in the past and see yourself continuing to use in the future. If your favourite is not here, write it in.

2. Circle the words that best correspond to Activities where you have experienced yourself having passion in the past. If your favourite activity is not here, write it in.

Channels	Activities
visual arts	drawing
crafts	constructing
music	doing crafts
manual trades	fixing
equipment	cooking
wood	making music
metal	producing
	gardening
	speaking
	tending animals
	writing

3. Now, define the words you have circled or written in with a sentence.

Summing up . . .

Take a few minutes to write down any thoughts you may have at this point in exploring your PRISM:

Appendix C
Companions on the Journey

When doing ministry, it is important to work with those with whom we can identify. We know when we are with the right people, in the right situation, when we find our passion released, our caring deepened, our commitment strengthened, and our energy flowing effortlessly and freely. Place a check mark beside the group size or type or group where you find your energy released and commitment strengthened.

☐ *Individuals*: Relating in a one-to-one situation.

☐ *Small groups*: gatherings of between 2 and 12 people, the group size that allows for mutual support and deep sharing.

☐ *Family size*: gatherings of up to 50 persons, the size of an extended family. People know each other well, and are there for each other when needed.

☐ *Fellowship groups*: gatherings of up to 150 persons, the size of the majority of congregations, a group where personal leadership can be exercised.

☐ *Assembly*: larger gathering of over 150 persons where one projects leadership and relates in more symbolic ways.

☐ *Men*: a preference for working with men only.

☐ *Women*: a preference for working with women only.

☐ *Mixed groups*: a preference for working with mixed groups of men and women.

☐ *Children*: a fondness for the excitement and energy that working with children entails.

☐ *Youth*: those working with youth cherish the opportunity to share in this stage when teens are looking for models and discovering their identity.

☐ *Young adults*: working with people in the 18 to 24 year age group — completing their education, considering work options, and often looking for life partners.

☐ *Adults*: persons 25 and up, some of course more adult than others.

☐ *Seniors*: the 65-75, 75-80, and over 80's constitute three sub-groups, each with different needs and different focus.

[ ] *Healthy situations*: some of us prefer to work in situations with individuals who are mature and doing well.

[ ] *Illness*: caregivers and the empathetic provide for the special needs of those who are ill.

[ ] *Conflict*: stepping into a conflict situation requires special skills and a zest for finding a way through difficulty.

[ ] *Powerless*: standing with the powerless and disadvantaged, the marginalized.

[ ] *Powerful*: the power brokers and leaders of society are often people who welcome support and additional insight.

Who are the Companions your intuitions say you are most likely to find intense satisfaction walking beside in life?

Appendix D
Community Opportunities

A list below names eleven types categories of communities: the Arts, Church, Home, Extended Family, Friends, Neighbourhood, Athletics, Recreation, School, Work, and the World.

Step 1.   Beside each category, list the key communities to which you belong, ones where you play a major role or know a significant number of people.

Step 2.   When you have entered your key communities, evaluate each by putting a check mark (√) in the column to indicate:
  √   communities to which you have **access**. We are thinking here of physical access, being a member, having geographic proximity.
  √   communities which are **open** to you using your gifts, particularly those providing an opportunity for you to use your gifts in ministry.
  √   communities where there is a **need** for your gifts.
  √   communities where you have a **passion** and would feel comfortable working — communities where you have a sense of belonging and of being included.

Communities	1. Particular Communities You Belong To	2. Evaluate Your Communities			
		Access	Open-ness	Need	Passion
Arts					
Church					
Home					
Extended Family					

Communities	1. Particular Communities You Belong To	2. Evaluate Your Communities			
		Access	Open-	Need	Passion
My Friends					
Neighbourhood					
Athletics					
Recreation					
School					
Work					
World					

Name the three communities where you have the most check marks.

1. _____

2. _____

3. _____

Appendix E
Your Personal Prism

Circle all the categories that apply to you:

Gifts which are your strengths	Areas that release passion	Channels you prefer	Companions on the Journey	Key Communities
Leadership	People	Write in your preferred Channels:	Individuals	Circle your key Categories:
Planning			Small groups (2-12)	Arts
Communicating				Church
Caring			Family size (up to 50)	Home
Discernment	Information			Extended Family
Spirituality			Fellowships (to 150)	Friends
Mentoring			Assembly (over 150)	Neighbourhood
Artistic Creativity	Skills	**Activities** that energize you	Men Women Mixed groups	Athletics Recreation School Work World
		Your preferred Activities:	Children Youth Young adults Adults Seniors	*Write in your key particular communities:*
			Healthy situations Illness Conflict	
			Powerless Powerful	

Putting It All Together

Write a paragraph describing yourself, based on the information you have discerned so far. Include:

- Your top two or three gifts as revealed by the Spiritual Gifts Instrument.
- The Area in which you prefer to work, whether with People, Information or Skills.
- What makes accomplishments special for you?
- The Channels you prefer.
- The Activities in which you experience the most passion.
- The Companions on the Journey with whom you feel most energized.
- The communities where you currently have the greatest opportunities to use your gifts.

Appendix F
Exploring Gifts as a Group

The following outlines a session that can be used with a small group. The object is to provide an occasion where each person can explore their individual gifts, and the group can develop a picture of how those gifts could fit together to improve the group's ability to do its chosen task.

Opening: Open by lighting the Christ candle and sharing a prayer together. Each member can then light their candle in memory of someone who has been important in their life. Or you can have people light candles when it is their turn to share their gifts.

The Gifts Chart: The Gifts Chart is a large circle on cardboard or newsprint that names the eight gifts. Have each person indicate his or her top two or three gifts on the chart. Colour in the section where a number of people have gifts in common. Then take a look at the chart and explore what it says to you. Where are your gifts concentrated? Where are the gaps? What does the chart say about your group's task or your work together?

Sharing: Go around the circle with each person sharing their Prism. While sharing, you may want to have a stone, a "talking stick," a feather, or some other symbol to encourage communication. The person holding the symbol has the full attention of everyone else. When each person is finished sharing, the symbol is passed to the next person.

If the purpose is to help individuals identify ministries, take time to work with each individual. If the purpose is to help the group identify a ministry they might undertake in common, let that be the subject of sharing and discussion.

Exploring: Here is where you get information up on flip charts or newsprint. Ask people to identify whether they prefer to work with people, information, or skills, and record the information. Do some brainstorming to explore what that might mean for your work. Ask people to share the channel through which they prefer to work and the activities they have found best release their passion. Talk about the needs you know of in the community where the group is based, or in other communities where group members have contacts.

Closing: Give people an opportunity to extinguish their candles, perhaps sharing a prayer of thanks for the time spent together as they do so. You can give each participant their candle to take with them as well as a prism to use during times of personal reflection and prayer. Ask someone to pull the insights of the group together into a document that can serve as a guide for the group in the future.

Appendix G
What Jesus and Paul Say about Gifts

Paul

Paul sets the stage for our understanding of individual gifts in the life of the church. He stresses that our different gifts have the one source — God's Spirit.

> There are different kinds of spiritual gifts, but the same Spirit gives them. There are different ways of serving, but the same Lord is served. There are different abilities to perform service, but the same God gives ability to all for their particular service. The Spirit's presence is shown in some way in each person for the good of all. The Spirit gives one person a message full of wisdom, while to another person the same Spirit gives a message full of knowledge. One and the same Spirit gives faith to one person, while to another the power to heal. The Spirit gives one person the power to work miracles; to another, the gift of speaking God's message; and to yet another, the ability to tell the difference between gifts that come from the Spirit and those that do not. To one person the Spirit gives the ability to speak in strange tongues, and to another the ability to explain what is said. But it is one and the same Spirit who does all this; as God's Spirit wishes, a different gift is given to each person
> (I Corinthians 12:4-11 GNB).

In his letter to the church in Rome, Paul reminds them their unity lies in the fact that, like the parts of the human body, each person's gift is important to the welfare of the whole.

> We have many parts in the one body, and all these parts have different functions. In the same way, though we are many, we are one body in union with Christ, and we are all joined to each other as different parts of one body.
> So we are to use our different gifts in accordance with the grace that God has given us. If our gift is to speak God's message, we should do it according to the faith that we have; if it is to serve, we should serve; if it is to teach, we should teach; if it is to encourage others, we should do so.

Whoever shares with others should do it generously; whoever has authority should work hard; whoever shows kindness to others should do it cheerfully.

Love must be completely sincere. Hate what is evil, hold on to what is good. Love one another warmly as Christian brothers and sisters, and be eager to show respect for one another. Work hard and do not be lazy. Serve the Lord with a heart full of devotion. Let your hope keep you joyful, be patient in your troubles, and pray at all times. Share your belongings with your needy fellow Christians, and open your homes to strangers (Romans 12:4-13 GNB).

Notice how the gifts Paul names correspond to gifts we have identified:

❑ Communication: "If our gift is to speak God's message ... If it is to teach ..."

❑ Caring: "If it is to serve ... Whoever shares ... Whoever shows kindness ..."

❑ Leadership: "Whoever has authority ...

❑ Spirituality: "Love must be completely sincere ... Serve the Lord with a heart full of devotion."

❑ Mentoring: "If it is to encourage others ..."

Elsewhere Paul stresses the other three gifts:

❑ Planning: "You are God's building. Using the gift that God gave me, I did the work of an expert builder and laid the foundation, and another is building on it. But each one must be careful how they build" (1 Corinthians 3:10 GNB).

❑ Discernment: "Let God transform you inwardly by a complete change of your mind. Then you will know the will of God — what is good and is pleasing to God and is perfect" (Romans 12:2 GNB)

❑   Artistic Creativity: *Paul is an artist with words.* "I may be able to speak the
    languages of humans and even of angels, but if I have no love, my speech is
    no more than a noisy gong or a clanging bell" (I Corinthians 13:1 GNB).

Jesus

Each of the eight gifts are present in Jesus. That fact alone makes him very special.
He also comments on the gifts, encouraging their development in his followers.
Here are some of those passages.

Leadership

The key aspect of leadership is vision — leaders are guardians of the vision. Jesus
had an image in his mind he called "the Kingdom of God." A more accurate
translation today might be "the Realm of God" or "God's New Community." In
parable after parable, he held that vision before his followers.

> God's new community is like this. A woman takes some yeast and mixes it
> with a bushel of flour until the whole batch of dough rises (Luke 13:21
> GNB).

> Whoever wants to be first must take the last place of all and be the servant of
> all (Mark 9:35 GNB).

> God's New Community is like this. A man is looking for fine pearls, and when
> he finds one that is unusually fine, he goes and sells everything he has, and
> buys that pearl (Matthew 13:45 GNB).

Planning

Jesus had little patience with those who did not look ahead and plan for the future.

> If one of you is planning to build a tower, the first thing is to sit down and
> figure out what it will cost, to see if you have enough money to finish the
> job. If you don't have enough money, you may be able to lay the
> foundation, but will not be able to finish the tower; and all who see what
> happened will make fun of you (Luke 14:28-30 GNB).

Communicating

Jesus was the master of communication. His stories endure today. His parables still catch us off guard and challenge us to look at our relationships with others in a new day. Then there is his poetry, easy to remember, powerful in its simplicity.

> Happy are you poor;
> > the Kingdom of God is yours!
> Happy are you who are hungry now;
> > you will be filled!
> Happy are you who weep now;
> > you will laugh!
> > > (Luke 6:20-21 GNB)

Caring

Care for those who are less fortunate is a constant theme of Jesus' teaching. We think of the parable of the Good Samaritan as one outstanding example.

> Jesus concluded, "In your opinion, which one of these three acted like a neighbour toward the man attacked by the robbers?" The teacher of the Law answered, "The one who was kind to him." Jesus replied, "You go, then, and do the same." (Luke 10:36-37 GNB)

For Jesus, caring for others was doing God's work, creating treasure where it would never be lost.

> Sell all your belongings and give the money to the poor. Provide for yourselves purses that don't wear out, and save your riches in heaven, where they will never decrease (Luke 12:33 GNB).

Jesus' concern was not about whether people would be generous. That was taken for granted. The important thing was going about that caring in a way that honoured people and, in today's language, did not develop in them a welfare mentality.

> When you give something to a needy person, do not make a big show of it … When you help a needy person, do it in such a way that even your closest friend does not know about it (Matthew 6:2-3 GNB)

Discernment

Discovering the will of God took a great deal of Jesus' time. We read that immediately after his baptism, he spent a time in the desert area fasting, attempting to discern what kind of a "Son" he was being called to be (Luke 4:1-13 GNB). He was a person of prayer. He also called on those who would follow him to be equally adept at discernment.

> Jesus said to the people, "When you see a cloud coming up in the west, at once you say that it is going to rain — and it does. And when you feel the south wind blowing, you say that it is going to get hot — and it does. You can look at the earth and the sky and predict the weather; why, then, don't you know the meaning of this present time?" (Luke 12:54-56 GNB)

Spirituality

Prayer was a hallmark of Jesus ministry.

> Very early in the morning, long before daylight, Jesus got up and left the house. He went out of town to a lonely place, where he prayed (Mark 1:35 GNB).

He gave a prayer to his followers which we continue to use, discovering new insights as we mine its words for meaning.

> One day Jesus was praying in a certain place. When he had finished, one of his disciples said to him, "Lord, teach us to pray, just as John taught his disciples." Jesus said to them, "When you pray, say this:
> 'Father;
> May your holy name be honoured;
> may your Kingdom come.
> Give us day by day the food we need.
> Forgive us our sins,
> for we forgive everyone
> who does us wrong.
> And do not bring us to a test too hard to bear.'"
> (Luke 11:1-4 GNB)

Mentoring

Jesus chose 12 of his followers for intense mentoring. They were his disciples. We know from the way Jesus spoke to Peter that he looked for the potential in his followers and challenged them to develop their gifts to the fullest extent.

> Peter, you are a rock, and on this rock I will build my church, and not even death will ever be able to overcome it (Matthew 16:18 GNB).

Artistic Creativity

Jesus painted word pictures that reminded people of the spiritual lesson to be learned from ordinary everyday things — like birds, growth and clothing.

> Put away anxious thoughts about food and drink to keep you alive, and clothes to cover your body. Surely life is more than food, the body more than clothes.
> Look at the birds of the air; they do not sow and reap and store in barns, yet your heavenly Father feeds them. You are worth more than the birds!
> Are there any of you who by anxious thought can add a foot to their height?
> And why be anxious about clothes? Consider how the lilies grow in the fields; they do not work, they do not spin; and yet, I tell you, even Solomon in all his splendour was not attired like one of these. But if that is how God clothes the grass in the fields, which is there today, and tomorrow is thrown in the fire, will God not all the more clothe you (Matthew 6:25-30)?

Appendix H
Celebrating Gifts

In this Appendix, we offer two approaches to celebrating gifts. The first is for use by an individual who is using this resource to identify his or her gifts and potential for ministry. The second contains ideas a congregation can use to emphasize that its goal is to support individuals in their ministry as well as the ministries that the congregation undertakes corporately.

For Individuals

Find a comfortable location where you are free to move. Choose a piece of music that fits the gifts you have identified in yourself. Have writing paper and a pen, or if you prefer to draw, paper and coloured markers or pencils. Light a candle, if one is available. Find one item in your house that symbolizes each of the gifts you have identified as being your strengths, and place those in the centre of the room. If you have a significant other, invite him or her to share this time with you.

A Prayer:

> Source of all that is …
> I thank you for my gifts of _____ and _____.
> *I turn to the north*, the direction the compass points, the location of the pole star,
> and celebrate that you are my fixed star in a changing world,
> my guide, my sense of direction as I grow on my journey through life.
> *I turn to the east*, and remember it was Magi from the east who brought gifts of gold, frankincense and myrrh to honour Jesus at his birth.
> I celebrate that gifts are not gifts until they are given away,
> and I ask for guidance in that giving.
> *I turn to the south*, and think of the people of the Third World, so many of whom live in the southern hemisphere, but also of those who live in pockets of poverty in my country.
> Help me to find where my gifts are needed, and the courage to use them there.

I turn to the west, where the sun sets, creating a time for rest and renewal. May I be ever refreshed and energized as I give what I have to offer, and offer what I have to give.

Read this portion of Psalm 116 over twice:

How wonderful are your gifts to me;
how good they are!
I praise God who guides me,
in the night my conscience warns me.
I am always aware of God's presence;
My God is near, and nothing can shake me.
I am thankful and glad,
and I feel completely secure,
because you protect me from the power of death.
I have served you faithfully,
and you will not abandon me, even when I die.
You will show me the path that leads to life;
your presence fills me with joy
and brings me pleasure forever.

Spend three minutes just listening as the Psalm speaks to you.

Using your paper, write a prayer — or create a drawing — reflecting on your gifts and the potential that is in them for fulfilling your destiny and living out your call.

Closing

May the grace of our Creator surround you.
May the love of Christ warm your heart.
May you be held in the arms of God's Spirit today and forever.

For Congregations

There are many ways of celebrating the gifts of members of a congregation.

Prism Weekend

Plan a Prisms Weekend. A Friday night banquet or potluck supper is followed by short stories from eight people outlining how each of the eight gifts enriches their life and the lives of those around them. On Saturday morning hold a Prisms Workshop where people work through the process for a large group. A "Gifts Sunday" celebration could cap it all off.

Gifts Sunday

A "Gifts Sunday" is a worship event consisting of eight people who each give a short description of what it means to have one of the eight gifts. Follow each presentation with the singing of a verse or two of a hymn that celebrates that particular gift. Some suggestions for hymns are:
> Leadership: "Be Thou My Vision"
> Planning: "Seek Ye First the Kingdom of God"
> Communicating: "Draw the Circle Wide"
> Caring: "Amazing Grace"
> Discernment: "Come and Find the Quiet Centre" or "In the Bulb there is a Flower."
> Spirituality: "Come to the Well"
> Mentoring: "We are Pilgrims" (The Servant Song)
> Artistic Creativity: "Dance with the Spirit"

Finish with a presentation of how the congregation intends to support the people in the use of their gifts in ministry, both within the congregation and in the many other communities where there are opportunities for service.

Gift Celebration Sunday Series

Set aside eight weeks to celebrate the gifts of congregational members, the role they play in the life of the congregation, and the contribution they make using those gifts in other communities (family, work, recreation, extended family, etc).

Taking Gifts to Work

Honour the occupations represented in the congregation on special Sundays throughout the year. These are places where people spend a large portion of their time, and are a major place where gifts are put to work. Examples are the healing professions, office workers, retail, the food and restaurant industry, police and military, etc. On those Sundays, people from the occupation being honoured are asked to attend worship in the clothing they would normally wear to work. Symbols of the work are placed on the communion table. People from that group read the scripture, offer the prayers, give the message, or perform a sketch dramatizing the challenge of being a Christian in their line of service.

Communicant or Church Membership Class

Use the Prisms instruments and small group process with a communicant or church membership class in order to emphasis they are wanted for their particular gifts, and to learn what those gifts are so they can be supported in their use.

These are just a few ideas for celebrating people's gifts. You can probably think of others. We would love to hear what you have done in your congregation. Just send an e-mail to <joyceandclair@congregationallife.com>. We want good news to travel fast.

Works Cited

Abella, Irving, "Tales to restore your faith in humanity." Book review. *The Globe and Mail*, Section D, Saturday February 15, 2003.

Browning, Elisabeth Barrett, *Aurora Leigh*.

Conger, Jay A. and Associates, *Spirit at Work*. San Francisco: Jossey-Bass, 1994.

Lawson, Jim, "Leadership: the virtue that became a vice." *United Church Observer,* February 2003.
<http://www.ucobserver.org/archives/feb03_ministry.htm>

Moore, Thomas, *Care of the Soul*. New York: Harper Collins, 1993.

Newell, J. Philip, *Celtic Benediction*. Toronto: Novalis, 2000.

Oaks, Gordon (interview), "A Big Church Sets its Sights on Small," *Congregational Life Newsletter*, December 2002. Available on line at <www.congregationallife.com>.

Richardson, Jan L., *In Wisdom's Path: Discovering the Sacred in Every Season*. Cleveland, Ohio: The Pilgrim Press, 2000.

Russell, Mary Doria, *The Sparrow*. Toronto: Random House, 1966.

Spong, John, *A New Christianity for a New World*. San Francisco: HarperCollins, 2001.

Saunders, Clark & Clair Woodbury, *Ministry as an Art*. Toronto: The United Church Publishing House, 1996.

Walton, Clarence, *The Moral Manager*. Cambridge, Mass.: Ballinger, 1988.

Winfrey, Oprah. "What I know for sure." *The Oprah Magazine*. 12 Sept. 2003. p.286

Bibliography and Resources

Books

Ackerman, John, *Spiritual Awakening. A guide to spiritual life in congregations.*
Washington: The Alban Institute, 1994.
Deals with spiritual formation, leadership and discernment.

Baldwin, Christina, *Calling the Circle.* Mill Spring, NC: Swan Raven, 1994.
The primer on developing small groups that truly minister to people.

Diehl, William E., *Ministry in Daily Life. A practical guide for congregations.* Washington:
The Alban Institute, 1989.
A lay leader reveals what it means to develop lay leadership in a
congregation.

Easum, William M. and Thomas G. Bandy, *Growing Spiritual Redwoods.* Nashville:
Abingdon Press, 1997.
A how-to book on developing spiritual "giants."

Elliott, Charles, *Strategic Planning for Churches. An Appreciative Approach.* Matthews,
NC: Christian Ministry Resources, 1997.
A survey of factors to consider when undertaking a planning process in a
congregation.

Kirkpatrick, Thomas G., *Small Groups in the Church. A handbook for creating community.*
Washington: The Alban Institute, 1992.
A step-by-step guide to developing a small group ministry in a
congregation.

Morris, Danny E. and Charles M. Olsen, *Discerning God's Will Together.* Bethesda,
MD: The Alban Institute, 1997.
A guide to making decisions based on the question, "God, is this your
will?"

Olsen, Charles M., *Transforming Church Boards into communities of spiritual leaders.*
Washington: The Alban Institute, 1995.
Church Boards should operate as a worshipping community.

Ó Murchú, Diarmuid, *Reclaiming Spirituality*. New York: Crossroad Publishing, 1997.
This book breaks new ground in defining the spiritual hunger of our time.

Posterski, Donald C. and Garry Nelson, *Future Faith Churches*. Winfield, BC: Wood Lake Books, 1997.
The authors visited 14 thriving Canadian congregations and identify dynamics that contribute to the congregation's effectiveness.

Rendle, Gilbert R., *Leading Change in the Congregation. Spiritual and Organizational Tools for Leaders*. Bethesda, MD: The Alban Institute, 1998.

Ware, Corinne, *Discover your Spiritual Type. A guide to individual and congregational growth*. Washington: The Alban Institute, 1995.

Woodbury, Clair, *Looking for God*. Toronto: United Church Observer, 1983.
Although long out of print, this book has sections on the spiritual life, discerning God's will, and caring for one another and the earth.

Woodbury, Clair & Joyce Madsen, *Wings Like Eagles. How to be a Thriving Congregation in the 21st Century*. Edmonton: Congregational Life Centre, 2000.
The five dimensions of a thriving congregation are described: spirituality, identity, context, leadership and vision.

Internet Web Sites

Congregational Life Centre, Edmonton. <http://www.congregationallife.com>
Access to the Centre's newsletters, as well as information about books, resources, courses and the consulting services offered by the Centre.

Easum, Bandy & Associates. <http://www.easum.com/>
Many resources for church renewal from these well known US church consultants.

Revelations Book and Gift Cooperative, Edmonton.
<www.revelationsbookstore.com>
Explore the on-line catalogue for books that deal with main-line church issues.